Amazing but True
Fishing Tales

By Allan Zullo

Astonishing but True Golf Facts
Amazing but True Golf Facts

Amazing but True
Fishing Tales

Allan Zullo and Mara Bovsun

**Andrews McMeel
Publishing**

Kansas City

Book design by Pete Lippincott

04 05 06 07 08 BID 10 9 8 7 6 5 4 3 2 1

ISBN 0-7407-4209-4

Library of Congress Control Number: 2003112472

To the Manausa anglers,
Trent Senior, Trent Junior, Mike, Joe, Danny,
and Bo . . . and their angelfish, Mary Lou.

—A.Z.

To my mother, Selma,
for all those perch she cleaned and
cooked at the boathouse so long ago.

—M.B.

Contents

Acknowledgments

WE WISH TO THANK the many anglers, guides, boat captains, and outdoor writers who provided us with information and stories for this book. We are also grateful for the assistance of Doug Blodgett, world records administrator for the International Game Fish Association (IGFA).

Casting Off

IT SEEMS THAT THE TYPICAL ANGLER has as many fish stories as a snapper has scales. But sometimes separating fact from fiction can be difficult, like trying to gaff a great white. However, no matter how tall a tale you might hear, the truth in fishing is often more amazing than anything an angler could make up.

This book is a celebration of real people and events in the fishing world that we hope will astound, baffle, and amuse you. Like the angler who used his rod and reel to hook and save a drowning child . . . the fisherman who reeled in a record bluefin tuna after jumping into another boat when his fighting chair collapsed . . . the surfer who retrieved a broken rod and hauled in a forty-three-pound black drum fish . . . or the young man who caught a world-record catfish using Spam as bait.

In this book, the fishermen aren't the only ones in the spotlight. So are many famous and infamous fish. Take, for instance, the shark that literally coughed up evidence leading to a sensational murder trial . . . the largemouth bass that has its own statue and monument . . . the tarpon that kayoed a surfer . . . and a turbot that was caught, put in the refrigerator for fifteen hours, and still survived.

From mountain trout streams to pristine bass lakes, from the marlin-rich waters off Hawaii to the tarpon-laden waters in Florida, it's no wonder fishing remains America's most popular participatory sport. It's the pastime where the most amazing things can—and do—happen.

Finny Fights

Anglers' Strange Battles

WHEN HIS BOAT'S fishing chair crumpled while he was battling a world-record tuna nearly seven times his weight, a desperate angler jumped into another boat and into its fighting chair and reeled in his prize catch.

It happened on September 5, 1970, when Dr. Richard Hausknecht, a gynecologist and obstetrician from Riverdale, New York, was fishing aboard the *Galatea*, a thirty-six-foot Hatteras out of Montauk, Long Island, with his wife, son, and

Captain Joe Moore, who was hired to help the angler find giant tuna. They were drifting and chumming in calm seas about twelve miles south-southeast of Montauk Point. Hausknecht was using a 12/0 Penn reel, 130-pound test line, a Finnor Viscount rod, and whiting for bait.

"My bait was about seventy-five feet down," he recalled. "Joe saw a tuna hit some of the chum on the surface and told me to bring my bait up. At the thirty-five-foot depth, the fish struck." It would turn out to be a 985-pound giant bluefin tuna—a formidable opponent for the 143-pound angler, who had never hooked any tuna nearly that large.

Minutes into the fight, the gimbal—a swiveled socket that holds the rod butt—in Hausknecht's chair broke, and then the chair itself collapsed, forcing him to work on the fish by jamming the rod butt in his abdomen. That meant the light-welterweight angler himself bore the full pressure of the fish. His only support was having his fifteen-year-old son Michael hold on to the top of his straining shoulders. "When the chair broke, I thought there was nothing more I could do but cut the line," Hausknecht said.

However, Captain Moore, believing that the angler had hooked a possible world record, conjured up a daring plan. He got on the radio and made a desperate call to area fishermen to volunteer the use of their boat and its fighting chair so Hausknecht could carry on his battle.

"I had never heard of anyone going from one boat to another with a fish on the line," said Hausknecht. "But I was willing to give it a try. I knew I couldn't get any other kind of help and that I'd have to bring it in by myself."

A nearby sportfishing craft, the *Tom Cat*, owned by Max Hoffman of Freeport, Long Island, came to the rescue. After Hoffman quickly maneuvered alongside the *Galatea*,

Hausknecht put his reel in free spool and, keeping a firm grip on his rod, leaped onto the *Tom Cat*. Then he strapped himself into its fighting chair and resumed the struggle. More than two hours after he had set the hook, Hausknecht brought the fish to gaff.

"The real difficulty was getting the fish into the *Tom Cat* and then transferring it to my boat," said Hausknecht. "Thank goodness, there were three people on the *Tom Cat* to help us. My wife Ginny had to operate my boat and she did a great job.

"Joe was sure I had a record but I didn't realize it until it was weighed back at the marina."

At the time, the all-tackle record for the bluefin was 977 pounds, so his catch had set a new mark. The International Game Fish Association (IGFA), which certifies records, said that the organization had no restrictions against an angler switching from one boat to another. Unfortunately, Hausknecht picked the wrong year to break the record. Over the next three months, his catch was bested by four other anglers, three of them fishing off Prince Edward Island in Canada.

Said Hausknecht, "That was okay. After my experience, I really got hooked on sportfishing."

While battling to land a great white shark, four fishermen found themselves starring in their own version of the thriller *Jaws*—except it was all too real.

On the morning of November 10, 1980, the anglers headed out of Cape Town, South Africa, on the *Aletta*, a twenty-foot twin outboard, in search of shark that they planned to catch and sell to a fish processor. At about 9 A.M., they spotted a fourteen-foot great white, so they used a 2½-foot shark as bait. They put a hook through the small shark's dorsal fin and attached the hook's line to a plastic buoy that was two feet in diameter.

Seconds after throwing the bait shark overboard, the great white swallowed it in one gulp, then started swimming away, towing the buoy behind it. They followed the shark for an hour before Gustav Boettger, the thirty-seven-year-old captain, pulled his boat alongside and tried to gaff the monster.

"As soon as we got near, that shark came out of the water like an express train and in one savage bite destroyed the buoy," Boettger told reporters later. Then the great white dove, came back up, and rammed the boat, tilting it at a crazy angle.

Fisherman Clive Mason, thirty-one, dashed to the pump to start getting rid of the water in case the shark had punched a hole in the hull. "While I was still moving toward the pump, the shark reared out of the water and lunged at me," Mason recalled. "I was standing so close that I could see past its rows of teeth, and deep in its throat.

"The shark then bit the side of the boat and attacked the motors. It slammed into one of the outboards with such force that it broke all of its bottom teeth on the metal."

Fellow angler Sweis Olivier, twenty-six, was worried that the great white had seriously damaged the boat. "I knew that once our engines were disabled we would be at the shark's mercy, and I prayed to God the metal would stand up," he recalled.

In the frenzy of the attack, with the boat rocking wildly, Mason said he yelled to the others, "If I go in the water, knock me over the head so I won't know what the shark does to me."

But Boettger gunned the boat and sped a safe distance away, leaving the monster thrashing in the sea. They returned a half hour later and found the shark too exhausted to fight. They gaffed it without any further problems. Back on shore, the shark tipped the scales at over a thousand pounds.

Recalled the fourth fisherman, Keith Murrison, twenty-nine, "What happened to us was exactly like those scenes from *Jaws*. Even as it was happening, I couldn't help thinking, 'This is it. This is *Jaws*.'"

A Wyoming angler who hoped to land a few fish from the Snake River wound up landing a few punches instead—against a three-hundred-pound grizzly bear.

On April 15, 2001, Knn Bates (yes, that's how he spells his first name) of Dubois, Wyoming, was minding his own business on the river. In four casts he had caught four fish—two cutthroats that he had put on a stringer and two brown trout that he had released. He kept the stringer in the water where it wouldn't create a scent because he knew he was in bear country.

Angus M. Thuermer, Jr., coeditor of the *Jackson Hole News & Guide*, who interviewed Bates, wrote an account of the ordeal, which is excerpted here with his permission:

Bates was on the north bank of the Snake River when he heard a noise behind him. "I turned around and there was the bear," Bates recalled. "He was standing there popping his jaws and whining."

Bates, who has hunted bears all his life, was uncertain what the bruin's strange behavior signified. "I didn't know, but it wasn't good," he said of the bear's actions. "He seemed upset about something."

Figuring the grizzly was out for blood, Bates decided to drop his rod, pick up a couple of rocks, drop his creel, and walk slowly toward a nearby bridge at Flagg Ranch. "This bear to me was acting weird from the very beginning," Bates said. "He just started after me. Luckily he didn't make a big rush.

"The bear walked with an attitude of 'This is what I'm going to do and you ain't going to do nothing about it.' There's no way I was going to play dead.

"He walked over and batted my creel. Then he ran right up on the road and started out on the bridge after me."

Bates backed out to the middle of the bridge. "There wasn't any sense going further," he said. The bear came on. Bates said he doesn't swim well but decided he'd go over the side, anyway. He turned to climb over the rail of the bridge when the bear lunged and grabbed his coat by the arm. Bates had endured enough. He lashed out.

"I just spun and hit him in the mouth," he said. "I was trying to hit him in the nose. I hit him with everything I had. He let go and kind of sat back on his rump. It shocked me. I didn't think I could knock a bear down."

Bates, forty-eight, who said he weighs 260 pounds and is five feet ten inches tall, wasn't going to wait for a standing-eight count. He pulled a rock out of his pocket and beaned the bear on its head "as hard as I could throw." Now the bear figured he'd go do his thing somewhere else. He ambled toward the north end of the bridge. Bates hit him on the rump with another rock as a send-off.

But as the bear neared the end of the bridge, a car came toward the two from the north. A couple of Utah tourists were inside. "They just drove up and started pushing him right back across the bridge," Bates said. The angler was out of the frying pan but back in the fire. As the bear approached a second time, Bates climbed completely over the railing. He hung there, the bear growling at him, as the tourists drove up and asked what was going on.

"I would like to apologize to the guy for my language," Bates said. The visitors finally comprehended the situation, beeped the horn, revved the engine, and drove the bear across the bridge. But rather than come back to help Bates, they continued south toward Jackson. Bates climbed back over the rail and collapsed on the road. He saw the bear amble toward Jackson Lake.

"Once it was over, I just couldn't move," he said. His knuckles were bloody from hitting the bear, he said. He had a small wound from a single grizzly tooth on his arm.

After the bear was gone, the angler gathered his thoughts and then his gear. When he got to his rod, he discovered a twenty-three-inch cut-throat on the lure.

Five casts, five fish . . . and a bear.

Finny Fights

A grandmother who had never seen a live tuna before bagged a 755-pounder, but not without a fight that left her without any pants.

On September 2, 1973, Mrs. Beryl Wonson, of Gloucester, Massachusetts, was on a charter fishing boat off Cape Cod. Shortly after a giant fish hit her line, the woman was buckled into a harness, and the battle was on. All was going well until the harness began slipping down her back, forcing her pants down below her hips.

Grandma Wonson wanted to yank her pants back up, but she couldn't loosen her two-handed grip on the rod, so finally she said, "The hell with them." Then she wiggled until they fell to the floor of the boat, and she kicked them off.

"What a relief in all that heat and exercise," she told the Associated Press later. "I was down to my lace-trimmed bikini shorts and T-shirt. But I was really getting the hang of fighting that fish, and the whole performance was so hysterically funny it wasn't embarrassing—except to the men, and they were perfect gentlemen. They kept behind me, back of the chair, and looked the other way."

Only after the big tuna was gaffed did Grandma Wonson pull up her pants and laugh with the rest of her anglers.

A similar ignoble incident happened in 1994 to an angler aboard Captain Val Rich's sportfishing boat after hooking a ten-pound bonito off Santa Cruz Island, California.

"The guy was fighting it off the back of the boat when his pants fell down around his ankles," recalled the captain. "He was an older gentleman with white BVDs and white legs."

Rich didn't know what to do. Should he pull the man's pants up or man the gaff and get his fish aboard? "The guy says, 'To heck with my pants, get my fish,'" Rich recalled.

"He's waddling back and forth across the stern of the boat. Everyone was rolling on the deck, laughing so hard they couldn't even put their lines in the water. No one else was fishing."

The fisherman may have lost his dignity but he caught his fish.

No angler has ever experienced a battle quite as strange as Charles Naething.

At the turn of the century Naething was a world-class fisherman, a record holder, and an expert at landing tarpon. The New Yorker liked to brag about the season he caught twenty-five of the silver monsters off the Florida and Gulf coasts. In fact, he liked to brag about all his saltwater conquests whether others wanted to hear about them or not—and most didn't, especially at the New York Athletic Club.

In 1905, Fred Wells, one of NYAC's members, had had it up to the gills with Naething's boasts. Wells said it was no big deal for Naething to pull in a tarpon because the fish "is blind with unknown fear and suffering awful agony from the hook, and he has no means of knowing what his captor is going to do."

However, said Wells, who belonged to the club's famed swimming team and made a weekly six-mile swim around Gravesend Bay, "With a man on the end of the line, it is quite a different proposition. He is supposedly every bit as intelligent as the fisherman, and what is more, is under no pain. There is no one on earth, no matter what may be his strength and skill, who can reel in a man who is thoroughly familiar with the water and who keeps cool."

Naething scoffed at the notion. "I have landed two-hundred-pound tarpon in less than ten minutes, and I am convinced that there is no man in the world I can't land in much less time."

And, so, the Man-Fish Contest was spawned.

The rules were pretty basic: Naething could use his best gear and have an assistant and had twenty minutes to reel in Wells, who would be underwater in the club's 75 by 25-foot swim tank. Wells would be outfitted with a leather harness on his head that would be strapped under his chin. On top of the harness, at the back of his head, would be a little ring that swiveled, through which Naething's fishing line would already be attached to simulate the feel of a hooked fish. The angler and the "man-fish" would be on opposite ends of the tank. Wells could wriggle, dart, and thrash all he wanted, but he couldn't use his hands to touch the side of the tank or grasp the line.

On the night of the contest, February 25, 1905, the balconies overlooking the club's swim tank were packed "so full that you couldn't have pushed a darning needle in with a hydraulic press," reported the *New York World*. "Lithe-limbed, bright-eyed, lean-necked young fellows, with barrel chests and slim legs" were rooting for the "fish" while those who were plump, middle-aged, and smoking big black cigars represented the "rod-and-reel, private-car, tarpon-destroying division," said the paper.

Unfortunately, Wells was ill from rheumatism that night, so Jim Clark, the assistant to the athletic club's swim coach, agreed to be the substitute "man-fish." He was certainly qualified. Clark was known to pack his lunch in oiled silk, tie the bundle to his head, and swim five miles offshore to dine while rolling on the waves.

When the starting pistol was fired, Clark darted and dived around the tank until Naething's fishing rod was curved down to the surface. Naething braced himself, placed the butt of the rod into a big leather socket hanging from his belt, and held the line, described as "21-strand line that breaks at dead weight of 42 pounds." Clark kept thrashing in the water for three minutes but then Naething began reeling him in. The angler landed the "man-fish" in four minutes, nineteen seconds.

A year later Naething consented to another contest, this time with Fred Wells, who had fully recovered from his bout with rheumatism and felt strong from months of training. At the start of the gun, Wells thrashed, kicked, and stroked. Naething landed him in three minutes, twenty-five seconds.

Having reeled in many tuna while fishing from his thirty-foot boat, *Rosie*, Harry Alfandre of Long Island decided he needed a new challenge—trying to catch a tuna from a rowboat.

After the *Rosie* towed a rowboat far from shore off Montauk on August 12, 1950, Alfandre hopped into the smaller craft alone and began chumming. Minutes later, he hooked a big tuna. According to fellow anglers in nearby boats, there was some question as to whether Alfandre had the tuna or the tuna had Alfandre because the fish was towing his boat around the fleet of weekend fishermen.

Wrote Raymond R. Camp, the *New York Times* outdoor writer at the time, "Alfandre battled the tuna for three hours. He was prepared to handle the fish without help and brought along a flying gaff tied with rope. When he had maneuvered the big tuna alongside his frail craft, Alfandre made a sweep with the gaff, sinking the big gaff hook into the tuna's jaw. There was a flurry of water, foam, tuna, and Alfandre, and when things quieted down, the reel was singing and the angler was still in the rowboat.

"The fight continued for another half hour, and when the fish once more had been brought almost to the boat (or the boat almost to the fish), the line parted. Somewhere there is a tuna with a nice new gaff hook and several feet of [rope] hanging from his jaw.

"Alfandre admitted later that it might have posed a problem if the line hadn't parted, as getting the tuna into the boat might have resulted in crowding things a bit."

Angler Trent Manausa and his son Bo had an up-close-and-personal look at the harshness of the food chain.

In 1995, the Manausas, of Tallahassee, Florida, were fishing in the Gulf of Mexico, when Trent hooked a six-pound amberjack. After a good fight, he brought the fish alongside their boat. As Bo was about to gaff it, a three-foot barracuda grabbed the amberjack's tail and took off, peeling line until Trent could turn the fish around and bring it close to their boat.

Once again, Bo was ready to gaff it when a larger, six-foot barracuda swam into the picture, bit into the catch, and took off. Trent fought it for some time and managed to reel it near them. But then a twelve-foot bull shark blasted out from under the boat, swallowed the barracudas and what was left of the amberjack, and wound up getting itself hooked.

The shark raced off, almost emptying Trent's spool. Trent finally got the shark stopped and then engaged in a fierce battle that lasted for ninety minutes. At one point during the fight, Trent was getting so worn out he needed to take a breather so he handed the rod to his son, but the shark was almost too strong for Bo, a high school football player at the time. To give themselves a break, they put the rod into the rod holder, but they abandoned that idea a few minutes later when they heard the fiberglass in the gunnels crack under the pressure.

Meanwhile Bo was maneuvering the boat in an effort to keep the shark away from a steel tower that rose out of the water and was being used by the Air Force during the training of fighter pilots. But the bull shark was so powerful it pulled the boat until the creature slipped around the tower and broke the line.

Neither angler was too upset by the loss. "When it was all over, we were both glad the shark got off," Bo recalled. "What would we have done with a twelve-foot shark? We would've had to cut the line if we got it too close to us."

Added Trent, "I was beat."

They returned to port with a keen appreciation for Mother Nature's food chain.

When John Leonard and his brother Jim took their rowboat out on Jamaica Bay for a day of fishing, John hoped to nab one of the big sea turtles that frequented the waters off Brooklyn and often stole bait from weakfish lines. But on July 8, 1912, a sea turtle nabbed John.

The eighteen-year-old Brooklyn angler felt a powerful tug on his line while in their rowboat near Rockaway Inlet. According to the *New York Times* account, this is what happened next:

"Everything was going nicely for the fisherman, when suddenly the turtle sprang half out of the water, turned and started for the rowboat at railroad speed. Like the man who caught the wildcat unaided, but needed help to let it go, John had no alternative other than to cling to his line and try to reel it in.

"He shouted to his brother to keep the boat out of the turtle's way, and the other boy exercised all his watermanship, but the turtle reached the boat, dived under it, circled around, and started off, still at full speed on another tack, with the line wrapped several times around the legs of his would-be captor.

"'Hang on to him. You'll get him yet,' shouted John's brother encouragingly as John flopped over the side and was dragged feet first under water. He sped through the water like a racing motorboat. Mostly his feet rose a few inches above the surface as he kicked and thrashed about. It was seldom that he managed to get his head out of the water and then he devoted his entire energy to catching his breath. His brother rowed excitedly along some distance behind.

"Then the fisherman suddenly shot to the surface of the water and turned over on his back. With a piece of the snapped line still fast about his ankles, John swam to the rowboat, almost exhausted and thoroughly scared. Along with the turtle had gone his new rod and line, which he had bought expressly for [the fishing] trip."

You never know what is under the water trying to steal your catch.

In 1998, an angler aboard a sportfishing boat out of Morro Bay, California, had hooked a salmon. As he was reeling it in, a seal grabbed hold of the fish. Neither side would let go.

As the tug-of-war played out, the captain ordered all the other fishermen onboard to bring in their lines. He then steered his boat, full throttle, directly at the seal. "You could see the look on the seal's face," recalled crewmember Wayne Blicha. "He held on right until the last minute.

The seal finally let go and dove for the bottom. We got the fish, although it was a little chewed up."

Fighting a grouper can be tough enough for anglers on a charter boat, but fighting each other is another matter.

In 1992, two couples who didn't know each other met at the docks in Cabo San Lucas, Mexico, and agreed to share the cost of a charter boat, one of several owned by Guillermo "Memo" Gamio. Everything was going fine until a large grouper struck one of the lines.

"The guys started arguing over who gets to fight the fish," Gamio later told the *Los Angeles Times*. "And they start fighting with fists. They didn't care about the fish . . . Pow! Pow! Pow!

"The skipper says, 'Hey, take it easy. If you don't take it easy, I go back.' And they keep fighting so he turned the boat around. It's maybe half past seven in the morning. [The skipper] calls me by the radio and says, 'I'm coming back! Get the Marines ready! These guys are crazy. They're fighting all over and destroying everything in sight.'"

By the time the skipper docked the boat, the fighting had stopped. But once they stepped off the boat, they started duking it out again while their wives were begging for them to stop. The police arrived and threw the two men in jail. They weren't released until they had paid for the damage they caused on the boat. Said Gamio, "They should have just flipped a coin" to determine who got to fight the fish.

When Jonathan Porter and his bride went on their honeymoon to Bermuda, they returned totally exhausted, but not from what you might think.

It was from a four-hundred-pound blue marlin.

On June 10, 1965, the Porters, who were from New York City, and another honeymoon couple chartered the fishing boat *Sea Wolf*, captained by Russell Young out of Hamilton, Bermuda, hoping to snare a prize catch.

At 10:30 A.M., Porter got his wish when he set the hook on a feisty marlin. He strapped himself into the fighting chair and anticipated a spirited, lengthy battle. But he wasn't prepared for how lengthy it would be. Fish and angler engaged in a fierce struggle through the morning and afternoon and evening. His fellow anglers cheered him on time and again as he brought the marlin close to the boat, only to moan when the fish made another of more than a dozen strong runs.

As night fell, Porter and the others onboard were weary but no one wanted him to give up. They finished the last of the food and water, and everyone except Porter and Captain Young went to sleep. At daybreak, Porter was still battling the marlin, which by now had carried the *Sea Wolf* sixty miles from the first strike.

Unfortunately, the boat's radio wasn't working properly so no one back in Hamilton knew what had happened to the honeymooners. Authorities dispatched a Coast Guard cutter and search and rescue planes but they were unable to spot the *Sea Wolf*.

Meanwhile, Porter, who was as hungry and thirsty as the rest of the passengers, kept fighting the fish into the afternoon and early evening. He absolutely refused to give up, believing that he would soon land the marlin.

But then at 5:56 P.M., after a battle that raged for thirty-one hours and twenty-six minutes, it all came to an abrupt end. The line had broken. And so had Porter's heart.

As the dejected anglers headed home, a search plane managed to make contact with the boat. Speaking on his faulty radio, Captain Young said, "There are four people on this boat who want nothing more than a hot shower, a cold drink, and a good meal."

In its account of the fish that got away, United Press International said that Porter "mourned the loss of his fish [but] fortunately he still had a line secured to his wife."

An eight-hundred-pound tuna triggered a fierce battle between two competing groups of anglers who spent more time fighting each other for possession of the fish than in catching it.

It happened on September 16, 1985, when anglers on two boats temporarily hooked the tuna about thirteen miles off the coast of Gloucester, Massachusetts. Thomas Galgana and his brother Michael were aboard their boat, the *Michelle Lee*, when they hooked the tuna. Nearby, fishermen aboard the *Sea Hope 1* also had snared the same tuna.

Although the fish had two hooks in it, the Galganas managed to reel the tuna toward their own boat. The *Sea Hope 1* fishermen then headed toward the *Michelle Lee*, shouting that they had hooked the same tuna moments earlier but that the Galganas had stolen it from them.

According to authorities, when the brothers refused to give up the tuna, their boat was rammed by the *Sea Hope 1* and then boarded by a man who backed off when the brothers fired a flare into the air.

The *Sea Hope 1* followed the *Michelle Lee* twenty-six miles to Green Harbor in Marshfield, Massachusetts, where the Coast Guard, local police, and the state Marine Fisheries Division were called in to settle the dispute. Authorities ruled that the tuna belonged to the Galganas, who then sold it to a fishery for $3,350.

"This is a first," Thomas Galgana told reporters. "I've caught fish with hooks in them, but I've never had anyone chase me around town about it, claiming it was his hook."

When a New Zealand fisherman speared a large striped marlin, he took the wildest ride of his life.

On April 19, 1997, Chris Browne was competing in a spearfishing contest when he made a spur of the moment decision to spear a 295-pound marlin. The next thing he knew, he was aquaplaning at about ten miles an hour. He managed to keep his head above water, hanging on to a fifty-foot rubber cord, attached to the spear, which stretched as much as 150 feet while the marlin dragged him.

The speeding game fish, which dived to depths of sixty feet, towed Browne three miles out to sea. Then it turned and weaved back toward the shore near the Hen and Chicken Islands off New Zealand's northern coast, where it was finally caught.

"At one stage I was very dubious whether I could handle it," Browne told reporters later. "I was very lucky, really. I just hung on and once I realized he was starting to tire, I knew I had him."

Finny Fights

Some fish stories seem a little too fishy to believe, but every once in a while enough evidence surfaces to give it credibility. Here's such a tale from Oregon reported on bassfishingnetwork.com:

In the summer of 1934, Mitch Sanders and his wife Bea played host to his brother Matt and Matt's wife Sadie, who were visiting from back East. One day, the four of them rode in Mitch's Model T Ford to one of his favorite fishing spots on the Columbia River near the mouth of the Pacific. It was there where Mitch decided to pull a little joke.

The men unloaded the car and made sure the ladies were comfortable with their basket lunch and sun umbrellas. Then the men set out to fish. After handing Matt a couple of bamboo poles and a can of worms, Mitch took out of the trunk a seventy-five-foot-long rope attached to a makeshift hay hook that resembled a giant fish hook. Next, he reached into an old canvas bag and pulled out a dead chicken, which he skewered onto his oversized hook. Finally, he tied the loose end of the rope to a length of chain that he attached to the bumper of his Model T.

Looking on in bewilderment, Matt blurted, "What are you doing?"

Mitch replied, "This fine river contains some of the largest fish in the world, and this is a common way to catch the big ones in these parts."

"You're full of it," Matt countered. "There's no way there are any fish in this river that could swallow that chicken."

"Oh yes, there are," declared Mitch. He spun the rope like a lasso and the chicken splashed into the water with the rope that remained attached to the chain, which was still wrapped around the car bumper. Then they plopped down for a relaxing day of fishing with poles and worms rather than Mitch's exaggerated fishing technique.

Eventually, the fast current pulled the rope near the
shore in about five feet of water leaving the hooked chicken
bait bobbing up and down a few yards directly in front of the
anglers. As they began laughing, Matt shouted, "What is
that?" He pointed to a bulge in the water, heading directly
toward them at a high rate of speed. Suddenly the mysterious
bulge broke the surface, allowing them to see that it was an
incredibly huge fish. Spinning on its side and exposing its
monstrous tubular mouth, the fish inhaled the chicken bait
in one great chomp. It then drenched the stunned anglers
with a splash, whipped around, and zoomed seaward.

The fishermen stood aghast, not knowing for sure what
had happened when shouts from their wives brought the
men out of their state of shock. They looked up to see the
rope grow taut and Mitch's Model T getting jerked toward
the river. The monster, with the huge hook in its mouth,

had leaped into the air and come down with such force that it had pulled the car's rear wheels onto the bank and then into eight inches of water.

The creature kept yanking the car farther into the river so that the rope was underwater and only the chain to the bumper was exposed. Having tied the rope to the chain instead of directly to the bumper, Mitch was unable to cut the rope. Seeing that he had little time left before his entire car was submerged, he ordered everyone into the backseat of the car for traction and hurriedly jammed the car in low and began to spin river rock under his tires. The car didn't gain any ground but at least Mitch had stopped its descent to the river bottom.

With the women screaming and the men hollering, the tug-of-war between fish and car continued for about ten minutes. It finally came to an end with a great popping sound when the bumper of the Model T was ripped loose and hurled through the air as though shot by a giant sling-shot, landing in the river with a great splash.

Mitch managed to drive his now bumperless car out of the water and back on dry land. As the four got out of the vehicle and stood on the riverbank, they watched in silence as the great beast broke the surface with one final leap before vanishing forever except in their memory.

Years later Mitch Sanders reportedly said, "I shared this experience with anyone who would listen. Some would scoff and some would laugh but the old-timers who lived along that river nodded with a look in their eye that let me know they believed me as they had seen these rare but huge sturgeon during their life on the river." Stories and photos of 20-foot-long, 1,500-pound sturgeon were not uncommon.

Eventually over time, Mitch, Bea, Matt, and Sadie passed away and their story was all but forgotten or written off as a tall fish tale.

But then in 1955, a dredger working the river bottom near the mouth of the Columbia raised the bumper of a Model T with a chain and rope attached to it. At the end of the rope was what appeared to be a hay hook that was pulled nearly straight. The dredgers were about to pitch it overboard as a piece of junk when one of the crewmen on board stopped them. Having heard Mitch Sanders's tale years earlier, the man related the story to his fellow crew members. Adding believability to this account, a license plate was still attached to the old bumper. It was dated December 31, 1933, and the first three numbers could still be made out, 491—which matched the first three numbers on the old Model T Ford of Mitch Sanders.

By Hook or by Crook

Weird Ways Fish Were Caught

SURFER TIM EBAUGH went out catching waves and wound up catching a big fish.

On August 7, 1998, Ebaugh, of Melbourne, Florida, was surfing along the Sebastian Inlet, at the southern end of Brevard County. He had just ridden a wave into the shore-break, nearly crashing his surfboard into the jagged rocks of the jetty, when he heard a woman angler yell from the jetty.

It was Helen Manion, a tourist from Delaware, whose fishing rod had catapulted over the railing and into the surf.

An experienced fisherman as well as surfer, Ebaugh paddled hard on his board, hoping to retrieve the rod. He intercepted the pole as it sliced through the water in front of him and he held fast to the reel. He quickly realized that there was a fish—a big one—on the end of the line because a powerful force was pulling him away through the breakers while surfers laughed and Helen shouted.

At first, Ebaugh was concerned that he was tangling with a shark because central Florida beaches are notorious for sharks. But because the fish never surfaced—unlike sharks, which usually come to the surface when hooked— he figured he was not in mortal danger.

After Ebaugh was dragged on his board for about fifty yards, the line went limp, so he sat up and furiously began reeling in the slack. The fish ran again, abruptly spinning him 180 degrees just as a large wave reared its foamy head and knocked Ebaugh from his surfboard. When he popped to the surface, Ebaugh was still hanging on to the rod, and was now only about twenty feet from shore. The rod had broken and, along with the monofilament, was entangled with his surfboard leash.

Worn out and bleeding from cuts on his leg caused by the line, he managed to bring to the shore his surfboard, twisted leash, and Helen's broken fishing pole. Once on the sand, Ebaugh reeled in Helen's catch—a forty-three-pound black drum fish.

"When I first dragged the fish to shore, she was still on the jetty, hand over her mouth, yelling, 'Oh my God! Oh my God!'" he recalled. "She came down to where I was on the beach, staring dumbfounded at the big fish, and, bless her heart, her first words to me were, 'Are you hurt?' I was still shaking from both the struggle and the excitement, and the fishing line had cut my leg pretty good. I told her I was fine but her rod and reel had seen better days.

"She asked me what kind of fish it was, so I told her. Then she asked, 'Whose fish is it?' I nearly died laughing at that one.

"I filleted the beast right there at the inlet and we both kept some and gave some away to onlookers. It was a lot of meat. It was something else."

Clark Stevenson swept his way to an Arkansas state record—literally.

On December 15, 1997, Stevenson and a fishing buddy were going after smallmouth bass at Greers Ferry Lake in north-central Arkansas. Late in the day, Stevenson hooked a hefty lake trout, reeled it in, and weighed it. The scale read eleven pounds, five ounces. But because neither angler liked to eat trout, they put it back into the water, hoping it would make it. The fish settled in shallow water near the Devil's Fork launch site.

Later that evening, Stevenson received a call from his buddy, who had checked the Arkansas record for lake trout and told Stevenson his catch far outweighed the record of eight pounds, one ounce.

Rather than kick himself for throwing back a state record, Stevenson grabbed a flashlight and an old push broom and drove back to Devil's Fork in the slim chance that the fish was still where he had last seen it. To his joy, the fish hadn't moved, and was resting in the shallows near the ramp. So Stevenson used his broom and swept it toward him and then caught it for the second time.

The next day the Arkansas Game and Fish Commission confirmed Stevenson had set a new state record for lake trout. As for the tackle, he got credit for using a Gitzit imitation crawfish and not the flashlight and broom.

Rats for bait? It worked for John Mina.

In June 2003, Mina, a podiatrist and adventurer from Alva, Florida, journeyed by plane, truck, and horseback to the desolate Egiin River in Mongolia to fish for taimen—the world's largest trout, which reportedly grow up to two-hundred pounds.

For the trip, he brought along rat traps because he had learned on previous expeditions to Mongolia that the natives use dead rats, or more accurately Mongolian ground squirrels, to catch taimen. Mina figured live rats would be better. But the critters didn't like the peanut butter he used for bait so his driver pulled out a .22 caliber rifle and shot the rats for the angler.

Following the advice of the natives, Mina fished at night using eighty-pound test and made a lot of splashing sounds, holding his bait of a dead rat on the surface in the current of the crystal clear, glacial-melt river. "I think I hooked the same fish four times," Mina later told the *Fort Meyers News-Press.* "He'd grab it, I'd try letting him eat, I'd set the hook, fight him, and then he'd spit it out. The last time he hit it, he was real close to shore. It was our last night and I was infuriated at that point. He grabbed it and I ran backward until he was about two feet out of the water. When he realized that, he let go of the rat again, but I ran up and grabbed him. I actually was in the middle of a herd of yaks when that happened."

Mina caught a 14-pounder and a 5½-pounder. "It was really exciting," Mina said. "They fought hard—a lot harder than a bass."

Despite being in a remote part of the world, Mina was well prepared to document the catch. He brought along a hand scale previously certified by the IGFA to weigh his catch and a video camera and a digital camera to record the event. He also had the fish certified on the spot as a taimen by the expedition leader, who held a doctorate degree in zoology. Mina hoped he had set a record.

But the IGFA rejected his bid for a world record because he used a mammal for bait, which automatically disqualifies the catch from official certification. Oh, rats!

By Hook or by Crook

An angler caught a bass thanks to a bolt out of the blue.

On August 11, 1913, Police Sergeant Michael Murphy, of West Orange, New Jersey, was fishing on the banks of the Passaic River with four friends. They had hooked pickerel, suckers, and sunfish, but no bass.

Murphy proposed to his pals that they each throw a dollar into the pot and the first one to catch a bass would take the money. The others were game, but after two hours of fruitless angling, they gave up because it started to rain.

While they ran to a nearby shelter, Murphy tried one more cast. To his good fortune, he got a bite and reeled in a beautiful big bass. Just as he landed it on the bank, his line broke. Given a new chance at life, the bass rapidly wiggled its way back toward its native element with Murphy in hot pursuit.

The bass was only inches away from the water, putting every ounce of its strength into one last flip to freedom, when a bolt of lightning struck it dead.

Murphy won the $5.00 pool.

Patrick Coffey returned home with a nice four-pound, five-ounce black bass. But he didn't really catch it. His dog did.

As friends gathered around Coffey in the town restaurant in Bloomfield, New Jersey, on August 3, 1907, the angler hung the bass, which was on a stringer, on a wall and told his story:

"I was fishing along the southern side of Oakes Pond without more than a weak strike every now and then. But I kept my eyes open, and pretty soon I saw something moving below the surface of the water about ten feet out."

By Hook or by Crook

Coffey was interrupted when Rover, his faithful
Newfoundland, which had been sitting by his side, began
howling and then lunged for the bass hanging on the wall.
The dog snatched the bass and ran with it out into the
middle of the street, wagged his tail, and then returned
to the restaurant, laying the fish at his master's feet.

"Gentlemen," said Coffey, "you see the antics of this
intelligent animal. Now, I didn't want to tell you fellows the
truth, not wishing to be put down as a nature faker. But my
conscience and Rover have determined me. I must tell the
truth, so here goes.

"What Rover did just now, he did this afternoon. Rover
caught the fish. As I said, I was fishing when I saw something moving beneath the surface, and Rover saw it too. As
we stood looking at it, this big bass leaped out of the water.
Before it could get back in, Rover had leaped with one

bound to the fish and caught it in his mouth. Then he swam back to me with the fish. That's the truth."

The story was told in the *New York Times* with a headline that read, A JERSEY FISH STORY CORROBORATED BY MR. COFFEY'S INTELLIGENT ROVER.

On the last day of duck hunting season near Caldwell, Idaho, on December 20, 1951, Gene Odle shot a teal duck that was flying over the Boise River. He sent his dog, a spaniel, into the water to retrieve the duck. Back came the dog in record time. But at Odle's feet, the dog laid, not a duck, but a twenty-seven-inch fish.

What started out as a bad day for a teenage fly fisherman turned into a remarkable turn of good luck.

In 2000, the angler, identified only as Mark, was fishing at a lake at Amherst Lodge in West Dorset, England, when he tempted a trout. Unfortunately, Mark's braided loop wasn't attached to his fly line properly and the fish swam off with his fly, leader, and braided loop. With a new fly, attached properly this time, he tried again. Amazingly, he caught the exact same fish and successfully brought it into the bank—only to discover that he hadn't hooked the fish a second time, he had hooked his braided loop.

Angler Lee Carver had to swim after the one that got away—and finally caught it.

During a contest at Barford Lake near Norwich, England, on June 23, 2002, Carver hooked a ten-pound carp. "When I first caught the carp, it was on the line for about five minutes before the rod broke and it got away," the fisherman told the *Daily Mail*. "I then had to watch as the carp towed my pole around the lake for more than three hours. I had to wait until the end of the match to try to get it back because I didn't want to scare the fish away from the other anglers."

In the meantime, he used a replacement rod and wound up winning the competition. Then he stripped to his shorts and swam after the finny escapee. About forty feet from the bank, he found the remains of his original fishing rod and realized that the carp was still on the end of it.

"It was a real scrap," he recalled. "I started swimming back to the bank, but the carp was still trying to get away and it was not easy swimming with one hand and holding the rod with the other one."

He climbed onto a jetty and eventually landed the carp with the help of a friend who had a net. Carver then let the fish go. "It was still alive and raring to go, so it seemed the right thing to do," he said. "It was certainly a tough old thing."

Anglers are a special breed, an ardent group of men and women who share a strong bond and are willing to go to great lengths to help a fellow fisherman.

Take, for instance, that day in 1989 at north Florida's Orange Lake when an angler on the bank had hooked a fish only to see a big old lake snake swallow the catch whole. Here's how James F. Burns, a professor at the University of Florida, described what happened next:

"Entering our unfolding daytime drama at this point was a big burly fellow, one of those fearless outdoorsmen who probably wrestle alligators for exercise and eat armadillo omelets for breakfast. Call him Burly Bob—being a man of motion and action, not words, he didn't give his name.

"The first thing he did was step forward and say, 'I'll get your fish!' And then, almost joyfully and with a whoop, he waded right into Orange Lake and seized that slimy, thrashing serpent with his bare hands. Everyone back on the bank was standing there, stunned and wide-eyed, watching this wizard of the water work his manly magic.

By Hook or by Crook

"Burly Bob quickly energized and animated the crowd of onlookers by hurling the snake onto the bank, virtually into the midst of the kids who had been cavorting carefree a moment earlier. Kids dived in all directions, except into the lake. All other routes were fair game, and the snake soon found itself alone and isolated on the bank.

"But not for long. Burly Bob waded up out of the water, a man on a mission. Grunting and dripping and smiling, he walked right up to his slimy, slithering prey. And, like a dentist after a molar, he grabbed the snake in one hand and the fishing line in the other and gave a big yank. Out popped the fish. The frightened but fascinated onlookers stared in amazement. They probably wanted to applaud Burly Bob's implausible feat, but found their hands trembling too much to make much noise.

"Satisfied that he had done the right thing, Burly Bob threw the snake back into the lake and sauntered off, leaving the fish for the fellow who had first caught it."

Harry Smith of Cleveland was fishing for bass near Midland, Ontario, on August 6, 1935, when he hooked a 1½-pounder. As he reeled the bass in, a large muskie seized his catch and swallowed the bass whole.

Smith didn't care about the muskie; he wanted that bass. It took him thirty-five minutes to land the muskie, and after he did, he extracted the bass and threw the muskie back into the water.

By Hook or by Crook

A fisherman landed two large tunas on one line.

It happened on July 26, 1938. William McTavish, a professor at New York University, was trolling for tuna with friends off Long Island on the schooner *Julieanna*.

He had a line off the stern of the boat when suddenly he felt two violent tugs. As he reeled in the line, he and his buddies let out shouts of surprise. Attached to his pork-baited hook was a tuna . . . and wrapped up in the line, about fifteen feet above the leader, was another, even bigger, tuna.

"After I got my first strike, I started to push up the rod to let the hook sink in, and then I felt another strike," McTavish recalled. "After the second strike, it was almost impossible to reel in. I thought I had a whale on my hook, and some of my friends began kidding me about it.

"As I reeled it in, though, I saw something tangled up in the line and it turned out to be a tuna that had accidentally been lassoed around the small of the tail, the cord having formed a half-inch hitch and cut into the tail. That tuna turned out to be a sixty-three-pounder, the largest we caught in a whole day of fishing.

"Then came the second one, about a fifty-pounder. You should have seen the look on the captain's face when he gaffed that lassoed fish."

A British angler has given credit to rap superstar Eminem for helping him catch more fish.

Mark Elmer, of Birmingham, England, told the *Sun* in 2002 that he took his boom box to a lake where he played tracks from the album *The Eminem Show*—and the fish started biting immediately.

Elmer said he hadn't been catching much fish in a lake near Chelmsley Wood. "I took my stereo to the lake because I hadn't had much luck recently. I wasn't worried about scaring the fish, but inside of the first ten minutes I had three or four bites and then I landed a whopping five-pound tench.

"I've never been the greatest fisherman, but now I'm catching them by the bucket-load."

Rodney Coldron, of Britain's National Federation of Anglers, told the paper, "I've never heard of anything like this, but I've no doubt playing music to fish could help catch them. Mind you, if everyone started playing music on the bank, it could have the opposite effect and scare the fish away."

A fisherman aimlessly throwing his jig in the water got a bite and reeled in a catch that was a double surprise—two bass on one hook.

While fishing in Maryland's Smoot Bay in 1988, Ed Loughran, of Mechanicsville, Virginia, was casting along one of the beds where bass spawn. "I got my jig close to a bed," he recalled. "A bass flared his gills and took the bait in, but when he sucked in the jig, it went through his gill and came out the other side. Just then another bass grabbed the bait and I set the hook. When I began reeling it in, I saw that two fish were stuck together on one hook. The first bass was on the line from his mouth through his gill and was blocked from falling off by the other fish.

"Both were the same size fish, about two and a half pounds each. I just couldn't believe it—two on one hook."

Loughran, an avid fisherman, admits he's been lucky ever since he was six years old and catching fish with balloons.

By Hook or by Crook

Taken by his parents to a company picnic near Dulles Airport, the little boy got bored and went down to a pond. "I saw all kinds of a little bass and was annoyed I hadn't brought my rod," he recalled. Then he had an idea.

He got some balloons from a clown and popped them. Next, he tore off the remnants of each balloon until all that was left was the string tied to the balloon knot. Keeping hold of the string, he tossed the balloon knot into the water. Within seconds, bluegills were hitting his bait. "Every time I threw it in the water, a bluegill would eat it and I'd yank him out. It sure was fun for a six-year-old."

A five-year-old boy caught a fish with his finger.

On January 17, 1938, Frankie Tate, of Westerly, Rhode Island, was tired of skating on Blackbird Pond, so he cut a hole in the ice and shoved is hand into the frigid water to test the temperature. Seconds later, he yanked his hand out and let out a shriek—because an eight-ounce pickerel was hanging on to his forefinger.

Frankie had the pickerel for supper.

Six-year-old Tammie Estes of Broomfield, Colorado, was fishing with her parents in the Granby Reservoir one day in 1970 when she lost her lure. So she baited her hook with a bit of clover plucked from the bank. Moments later, she reeled in a 15½-inch rainbow trout.

By Hook or by Crook

Fifteen-year-old Mary Speed was crappie fishing and wound up with a prize blue catfish—on a broken rod.

On July 17, 2000, Mary was on Cedar Creek Lake in Texas fishing with ten-pound test line when a forty-nine-pound blue catfish bit her slab spoon. The light line held up, but the powerful fish broke her rod about fifteen minutes into a fight that lasted thirty-five minutes.

With the help of her father, veteran fishing outfitter Ron Speed of Malakoff, Texas, Mary hung on and managed to wrestle the tired catfish into a bass landing net and aboard their bass boat. "It was pretty amazing because the fish wrapped up in the brush three times and still didn't break the line," Speed told The *Dallas Morning News*. "I had to use the trolling motor to stay with the catfish. We landed the fish more than two-hundred yards from where Mary hooked it."

Her strange catch missed setting a lake record by two pounds.

An angler landed a 116-pound yellowfin tuna with his bare hands.

In 2000, the *Washington Times* reported that Bennie Keisler was surf-fishing on an Outer Banks beach in North Carolina when he reeled in a little fish, a Norfolk spot. To his amazement, a much bigger fish was following his catch and beached itself in water less than a foot deep. Keisler easily grabbed the tail and landed the huge tuna.

Inmates and the warden of the Louisiana State Penitentiary thought the fish they caught was definitely one for the record books. But the only problem was that it wasn't hooked with a rod and reel. They brought it in by hand.

The fish, an alligator gar, was spotted on the grounds of the maximum security prison farm in an overflowing ditch in the midst of a flood caused by remnants of tropical storm Allison on June 8, 2001. "We caught him with a hay string, like you bale hay with," Warden Burl Cain told reporters. "The inmates got a little old rope around his neck and dragged him out."

The gar measured six feet, nine inches, and weighed 164 pounds. "I called to see if it was a record," said Cain. "They said it had to be caught on a rod and reel."

According to the state Wildlife and Fisheries Department, it would have been the second biggest gar ever caught in Louisiana. The record is 179 pounds. Not that the inmates' catch would have counted anyway.

Golfer Lennie Learmouth went looking for a lost ball in a bunker during a round at England's Wetherby Golf Club in 1995, but instead he landed a forty-pound, forty-five-inch-long pike.

The huge fish apparently got stranded when recent storms had caused a nearby river to flood the course, including the bunkers. So Learmouth grabbed a rake and snagged the pike. "I'm always hooking on the golf course," he said later, "but this is ridiculous."

By Hook or by Crook

California Highway Patrol officer Alvin Yamaguchi caught the biggest fish of his life—while standing at an intersection in the Los Angeles suburb of Irvine.

After torrential rainfall had turned many of the city's streets into rivers on February 13, 1992, he and CHP officer Bill Grant were assigned to the flooded intersection of Irvine Boulevard and Lambert Road. Wearing knee-high rubber boots, the two were standing in the middle of the intersection directing drivers away from the closed streets.

Suddenly Grant shouted at Yamaguchi and pointed to a big fish that was swimming by him. Yamaguchi quickly scooped up the fish, a thirty-five-pound carp, and threw it on drier ground. Apparently, the fish came from a small reservoir in the hillside above Irvine that had overflowed onto the street.

Yamaguchi had his picture taken with the carp because, he said, none of his fellow officers would believe his whopper of a fish story.

Mother Nature blessed seafood lovers by creating an avalanche of fish on a California beach.

On November 12, 1911, three fishermen had just set their seines for smelt at Ostend, between Long Beach and Terminal Island, when they sighted a huge school of croakers heading directly for their nets. Unfortunately, a huge rogue wave was also taking direct aim at them.

The wave swept up the school and then crashed into the shore, flinging thousands of fish onto the beach. Hundreds of passersby rushed to the beach and gathered the flopping fish into wagons, buckets, sacks, and garbage cans.

The wave nearly drowned two of the fishermen who were knocked down and slammed underwater. When they finally staggered to shore, they found their companion happily shoveling fish into a wagon. "Look," he said. "I'm catching more fish on land than I've ever caught in the ocean."

By sheer accident, angler Oscar Godbout discovered a new lure for salmon—Boston baked beans.

On the rainy, cold morning of May 16, 1966, Godbout was trolling a Gray Ghost across a lake near Lee, Maine, without much success. He took a break to munch on a baked bean sandwich and watched a single bean fall from between the slices of bread into the water. The bean disappeared in the rolling swirl of water that marked a feeding salmon.

That's when Godbout had a brainstorm. He pulled in his line and impaled a bean on the point of the streamer hook.

He swung the boat in a wide circle and then put the fly back in the water. Moments later the rod tip doubled and a salmon came out of the water in a clean, beautiful jump.

When Godbout netted the fish, he noticed the fly had hooked solidly in the jaw—and the bean was still on. As he later recalled, "Now a problem arose. Should I try the same trick a second time? If I did and failed to hook another salmon, I could well lose faith in beans as an effective lure. I decided to let someone else do further research and headed the boat back to camp for some hot coffee."

Bennie Parker, of Mount Pleasant, Michigan, told the *Detroit Free Press* in 2001 that he has used Gummi Worms—the popular chewy, jiggly kids' candy—to catch salmon.

"I started using them by accident," Parker said. "We ran out of spawn. One of the kids had this candy with him. I looked at the color and figured, 'Why not?' I stuck some on and we caught fish. Now I always have some with me when I go salmon fishing. If all else fails, I try the Gummi Worms."

Each Gummi Worm has several colors along its four-inch length that are the same as those anglers use on spoons and egg flies. The candy also has a translucent quality similar to real salmon eggs and a sweet smell that can easily be detected by fish.

"The only problem with them is that they don't stay on the hook real well," said Parker, "especially in places where you snag up a lot. But they're so cheap you don't care."

In the 1930s, salami was the bait of choice for trout fishermen in New Hampshire.

According to an account in the *New York Times* on August 16, 1930, "Salami is the only bait for trout."

Angler Joseph Vicarisi reported that he caught fourteen trout in Silver Lake, New Hampshire, using salami. "When I left the lake, everybody up there was catching them with salami. They can't resist it. It makes their mouths water. And that's no baloney."

Many anglers swear that the smellier the bait the better when it comes to catching catfish. In fact, the rank and rotten bait has spawned a cottage industry that's raising a stink in the fishing world.

Jackie Hughes, of Plano, Texas, told the *Wall Street Journal* in 2002 that his "Bells of Hell" catfish bait is made from thirty-six pounds of rancid hog brains mixed with a gallon of bait fish. It smells so bad, he said, "that if you get it on your hands, you have to have your hands cut off."

He sets his hog-brain mix in a plastic tub in an empty pasture where he whips it with an electric paint stirrer. "It smells like you took a feed lot, poured sour milk on it, then buried it in an old shoe."

Danny King, a bait maker in Kingston, Oklahoma, said his combination of old cheese and minnow oil has a smell that will "knock the buzzards off a gut wagon."

Benny Roberts, of Decatur, Texas, makes a concoction of cheese, ground-up fish parts, garlic powder, and other secret ingredients and then lets it ferment for a year in a tin shed.

Although catfish eat insects and smaller fish and not decayed items, smelly bait does seem to work, according to Charles Berry, a fisheries professor at South Dakota State University. But when asked why it works, Berry told the *Journal,* "I guess you have to ask the catfish."

Holy Mackerel!

Famous and Infamous Fish

NO FISH HAS EVER RECEIVED more worldwide attention and affection than a bass named Leroy Brown. In fact, he's the only largemouth bass buried with his own marble statue.

The monument was erected by the angler who caught him—Tom Mann, one of America's most renowned fishermen and the owner of Tom Mann's Fish World in Eufaula, Alabama. When he hooked the then one-pound, one-year-old bass in Lake Eufaula in 1973 with a strawberry jelly worm lure, Mann noticed that the fish was different from other bass. The fish had intelligent eyes. So Mann put the bass in his forty-foot-long, thirty-eight-thousand-gallon aquarium and called him Leroy Brown.

Mann tested lures that he designed by dropping them into Leroy's spawning beds in the tank. That's when the angler knew the bass was gifted. Each time that a lure interested Leroy, the fish would carefully move the lure to the other side of the aquarium without biting the hook. "If he went for them, I knew they were good," said Mann. "Funny thing, though, he wouldn't let other fish near the lures, like he was protecting them. Another thing he did was if a limp fish appeared to be losing its will to live, Leroy would repeatedly 'bump' the fish until it resumed swimming.

"That fish ruled the tank—he absolutely controlled it," Mann added. "If other fish got in his way, he'd bump them."

Holy Mackerel!

As Mann's affection for his young fish grew, Leroy seemed to return the feelings. The fish soon learned to jump through a hoop and lie down outside the water and eat from Mann's hand. He gradually grew to more than six pounds, much heavier than most male bass.

"He was the smartest fish I ever knew," Mann declared. "It was a once-in-a-lifetime thing knowing a fish like Leroy Brown."

Mann told his big-name fishing buddies about his intelligent bass and soon Leroy became a tourist attraction. People from all over the world stopped in Eufaula to see the remarkable bass. "He was the Dale Earnhardt of the fish world. He had more press than any bass in the world. Germany, Japan, England, Zimbabwe, Australia—that fish was known all over the world. Sometimes I got jealous of him because he got more coverage than I did."

On March 18, 1981—eight years after Mann caught him—Leroy Brown died.

"As far as we can tell, Leroy died because he was exhausted from too much mating," Mann's daughter Sharon told reporters. "From the moment Daddy put him in the tank all the female fish would watch Leroy. It wasn't long before they were all coming to him to spawn." Although a normal, largemouth bass will spawn once or twice a season, Leroy once spawned eight times, she said.

The bass fishing community collectively mourned the loss of Leroy Brown. Alabama Governor Fob James declared the day to be one of mourning for all bass. Country music legends Hank Williams, Jr., Porter Wagoner, Jerry Reed, and Sonny James sent telegrams of sympathy to Mann.

On the shore of Lake Eufaula, a crowd of five hundred gathered for the funeral. The Eufaula High School band played a rendition of Jim Croce's "Bad, Bad Leroy Brown."

Holy Mackerel!

Bass fishing's greatest anglers were called on as pallbearers. With solemn faces, Jimmy Houston, Roland Martin, Randy Fite, John Powell, and nine others carried Leroy's body in a velvet-lined, Plano tackle box. Ray Scott, the founder of the Bass Anglers Sportsmen's Society, gave the eulogy.

Because of rain, the burial was postponed, so Mann put Leroy's coffin in the company freezer. But during the night, someone stole the coffin. Mann assumed it was for ransom, but when no one called, he put an ad in the paper offering a $10,000 reward for Leroy's return. A few weeks later, he received a call from a man who said he was at the airport in Tulsa, Oklahoma, and wanted the reward. But before Mann could get his name, the guy hung up. Mann called authorities at the airport to look for the coffin. The next day, a person from Braniff Airlines called and said, "We have a box back here that smells pretty bad." It was Leroy's coffin.

The coffin was returned and buried in Eufaula in a pond-side grove by Mann's Bait Company. "We never found out who stole the body," said Mann. "All these years later, and still no one has owned up to it.

"I'm just thankful to have known a fish that will be remembered well after I'm gone. Leroy will be talked about forever."

In a gesture of his affection for Leroy Brown, Mann had a marble monument made in Germany and shipped to Fish World. He paid $4,000 for the statue of his pet bass and the tombstone upon which it sits. The inscription reads: *"Most bass are just fish but Leroy Brown was something special."*

A largemouth bass apparently holds two of the top-ten big-bass world records.

Holy Mackerel!

While fishing on southern California's Dixon Lake on May 31, 2003, Jed Dickerson, of Carlsbad, California, caught and released a 21.7-pound largemouth bass, the fourth-heaviest on record in the world. It appears to have been the same bass that was caught in the same lake by big-bass hunter Mike Long on April 27, 2001, when he pulled in a 20.75-pounder, which at the time became the world's eighth heaviest. He had weighed it and taken pictures of it before releasing it.

"It's the same bass I released in 2001," Long declared to the *San Diego Union-Tribune*. "When I first saw it, I didn't think it was," but after comparing it to pictures of his history-making 2001 catch, "I could see that it had the same black dot on the right lower side of its cheek that mine did."

He added that his bass had "a whole bunch of the same identifying marks" as Dickerson's catch. "It's the same bass, just bigger now."

Dickerson's bass, a potential International Game Fish Association line-class, world-record catch on twenty-pound line, measured 28½ inches long and sported a 26¾-inch girth. Compared to Long's bass, Dickerson's catch had lost ¼ inch around its girth but was 1½ inches longer.

Dickerson said he had a premonition that he might catch a huge bass because he had fished the same lake the previous year in the last week of May when, among his catches, he reeled in three bass weighing between 11½ and 14½ pounds and lost a bass that was even bigger than his newsmaker of 2003.

Although Dixon Lake covers only seventy acres, it has produced two of the top nine bass ever caught in the world. Of course, the catches are suspected of being the same fish.

When Dickerson spotted the huge bass early in the morning, he fished for it. He waited patiently for forty-five minutes before enticing it to bite his eight-inch plastic trout imitation swimbait. It took the angler less than a minute to reel it in. "When I got it in the boat, I yelled, and I know everyone at the lake heard me."

He used twenty-pound P-Line, spooled on a Calcutta 400 reel, and a G-Loomis Muskie Light Bucktail rod.

After having the bass weighed and verified by a ranger and a game warden, Dickerson released the record bass later in the morning, and it swam away powerfully. "She swam straight out and down, which is good," he said.

Who knows. Maybe over time the fish will gain some more weight and get caught again for the third time and break that elusive world record which stands at 22.25 pounds.

"See," said Long, "catch and release works."

While fishing late one evening near his home in Christchurch, Dorset, England, on November 3, 2002, Mike Reeves reeled in a one-pound turbot and stuck it in a plastic bag. An hour later, he returned home and put the lifeless turbot into his refrigerator.

The next day, he took the fish out of the refrigerator to cook for lunch. As Reeves washed the turbot in the kitchen sink, he was shocked to discover that the fish was moving. Even though it had been out of the water for fifteen hours, it had not yet died.

"When I realized that it was still alive, I didn't have the heart to eat it," the retired delivery driver later told the *Sun*. He quickly placed the fish in a sink of cold water and then phoned the Blue Reef Aquarium in Portsmouth. A staff member came to the house and transported the fish to the aquarium, where it was put into a tank of salt water. The turbot, which the staff named Herbert, made a complete recovery, and was given a permanent home there.

Marine fish expert Dr. Paul Gainey told the *Sun*, "The time the fish was in the fridge slowed its metabolism, much like hibernation, and helped it survive. Also, it was in a plastic bag so it would have been in a moist environment, which is important."

Added Reeves, "Now that was a fish that really wanted to live."

One gray day in March 2000, Norwegian angler Harald Hauso caught a blind cod in the Hardanger fjord. He released the fish because it was too thin. He didn't think anything more about the cod until he found it in his net the following week. Once again, he let it go.

But the fish kept returning almost every week, and Hauso kept setting it free. "I felt sorry for it because it was blind in both eyes," he told the Norwegian newspaper *Aftenposten*. "He was too thin to eat and he was in bad condition."

Finally in late January 2001, after Hauso had caught the sightless cod for the fortieth time, he decided to give it a new home. The fish was taken on a 190-mile journey to Aaslesund's Atlantic Sea Park, where it was supposed to enjoy its remaining years in a happy, safe retirement. "It'll be a good place for him to be a pensioner," Hauso said at the time.

The cod, which the staff named Balder after the Norse god of peace and joy, was placed in a private pool with a short-sighted halibut known as Big Momma. At first Balder seemed depressed and failed to eat, but it soon became happy in its new home and enjoyed a daily diet of herring and shrimp.

But the cod's health began to deteriorate, so it underwent surgery in April. Unfortunately, Balder didn't survive.

Hauso took the news of Balder's passing philosophically. "I never even expected him to survive the trip to the sea park, so it was a blessing he could live this long," he told *Aftenposten*. He admitted he was a little sad that he didn't get the chance to visit the fish in its new surroundings before its death. "I think the cod may have died from kindness. He had lots of food after not being used to such a life of luxury."

A fish called Mary was the biggest—and arguably the most famous—freshwater fish of any species ever to swim in Britain's inland waters.

Mary was a male carp that reached a weight of fifty-six pounds, six ounces.

The carp was only ten inches long when he was introduced into a 120-acre lake in Wraysbury, Berkshire, England, in 1972. He grew to more than ten times the size of an average salmon.

Mary got his name after he was caught for the first time in 1987 when he weighed twenty-eight pounds. He was named after the girlfriend of the angler who caught him but couldn't determine the fish's sex. The name stuck. Because carp have individual scaling patterns and can easily be identified from one another, fishermen set out to catch Mary.

During each nine-month season, two or three anglers were lucky enough to catch and release Mary, tempting him with bait ranging from sweet corn to bread.

"He was a very large and powerful fish," said Ian Welch, manager of the lake where Mary lived. "You needed a strong line, big hooks, and lots of stamina to catch him. He would fight for up to an hour and a half before giving up."

In 1991, Mary weighed forty-five pounds, six ounces. The following year he became one of just three known carp living in the wild in Britain to top fifty pounds and had attained celebrity status. He was featured in articles throughout Great Britain and had an armada of fans that, thanks to the Internet, were from all over the world. "So many of the best anglers in the world have sat on that lake for ages desperate to catch her, ignoring everything else in life," said a veteran fisherman on the Web site of RMC Angling.

By 1996, Mary had become the biggest freshwater fish of any species to have grown naturally in the wild in Britain. His weight peaked two years later when he tipped the scales at fifty-six pounds, six ounces. But then a slow, natural decline set in.

On August 19, 2001, Mary died from a suspected heart attack. He was thirty-two years old. "We are all devastated," Welch told London's *Times*. "I, personally, am gutted."

Said the *Times:* "The news of Mary's death cast into mourning the vast, closed world of the carp-fishing brotherhood—tens of thousands of anglers so mesmerized by the challenge of Britain's most intelligent freshwater species that they will fish for nothing else."

Carp-fishing Web sites and magazines were inundated with tributes to the great fish. "Mary will be greatly missed by millions of anglers," said one. "Mary wasn't just a fish. Mary was the queen of all carp," said another, who would have been more accurate calling him the "king of all carp."

There have been plenty of instances of a catfish knocking a man down in the water, but there has been only one cat that ever floored three men at once—on land.

The ferocious 110-pound fish had no real name other than the "man-smashing finny fighter," a moniker bestowed on it by the *New York Evening Journal.*

It all began back in the summer of 1896 when a fisherman netted the catfish out of the Missouri River near Plattsmouth, Nebraska. It was so big and ornery, that rather than kill and eat it, the angler put it in a water tank and took it to the state fair in Omaha, Nebraska, where the catfish became a big attraction. But the furious fish nearly bankrupted its owner by smashing the wooden tank time and again until a stronger, more narrow tank was constructed. The owner made the tank narrow so that the catfish wouldn't have much of a chance to swing its tail with sufficient power to do any damage.

When the fair ended, the owner decided to donate the fish to the state hatchery. Because of its reputation as a fierce fighter, several precautions were taken to prevent anyone from getting hurt during the move. After putting a cloth over the fish's head, three men tried to lift the big-jawed leviathan out of the tank. Here's how the November 15, 1896, *Evening Journal* reported what happened next:

> They heaved right royally, and so did the fish. At last he had room according to his tail. Over went men and fish on the floor, and the number of revolutions the terrible tail made in a moment would put any respectable flywheel to shame. All heads rolled around the floor, the fish landing every time he struck. It was the prettiest fight Omaha ever witnessed . . .
>
> The more the fish struggled, the stronger and wilder he seemed to get. Presently his tail went sideways with a

swish. A second later John Meredith, of the State Fish Hatcheries, found himself up against the side of the building with three broken ribs. Superintendent O'Brien of the Hatcheries, went head over heels from a blow of that powerful tail on one of his eyes. State Fish Commissioner W. L. May never knew what hit him, because it came so quick and hard, but it drove him some distance along the floor . . .

Then the great big conquering fish began to tire and lay limp and apparently lifeless upon the floor. This was the coveted opportunity. One man went forward, and to show his courage, patted the fish. Then he turned in triumph, and then—well, then there was a sudden s-w-i-s-h and the man of courage went into space as if he had been inspired by a full-grown catapult. It was the tail again—the tail of the biggest fish Omaha ever saw.

There is an end to all things, and so, after a while, the fish capitulated, was wrapped in a blanket, and carried in triumph to the hatcheries. When they dumped him into a tank there, he deliberately sank to the bottom and refused to move. Whether it was sulks or exhaustion, no one knows.

The nameless catfish lived out its life in a tank with extra-heavy glass sides. For days at a time, it would appear to sulk and then suddenly it would roar to life, bashing the sides of the tank in a desperate effort to escape.

Said the *Evening Journal*, "It's beyond question that this is the only catfish ever caught in inland waters which has a record of knocking out three men on terra firma, and which has lived to be feared and at the same time admired by his human victims."

A shark that was caught and killed got even for his fate.

"I must be the first person in history to be attacked on dry land by a shark—and a dead one at that," mused Darren Smith, of Newquay, Cornwall, England.

On September 3, 2001, Smith, a chef at the Dolphin restaurant in Newquay, had picked up the seven-foot-long porbeagle shark and put it in his vehicle. On the way to the restaurant, Smith braked sharply and his hand got caught in the shark's mouth, severing an artery and almost slicing off his thumb.

He immediately drove to the hospital where he needed seventeen stitches. "I felt like an idiot," he later told the *Sun*. "The nurses couldn't stop laughing when I told them how it happened."

A tarpon jumped out of the water, hit a surfer in the head, and knocked him out cold.

It happened on April 24, 2001, when John "Casey" McDermott, twenty-two, of Edgewater, Florida, was surfing off New Smyrna Beach at a time when tarpon were swimming close to shore to spawn.

McDermott was just about to drop into a curl when a five-foot-long, hundred-pound tarpon flew into the air and knocked the surfer senseless.

A fellow surfer, Chuck Carter, thirty-five, was about two hundred feet away and saw the spooked tarpon KO McDermott. "I looked over just as he was going for a wave, and right out of the back of the wave this tarpon jumped about three feet."

Seconds later, McDermott's board was floating by itself. The surfer and fish were gone. "I thought he'd come up to the surface, but he didn't, so I paddled out there," Carter told the press later. "There was a cloud of blood in the water, and he was a couple of feet under, just limp."

McDermott was underwater for about twenty or thirty seconds and inhaled some saltwater before Carter pulled him to the surface. The injured surfer was bloodied and unconscious and started coughing up blood. "I got him on my board and started paddling him in and just kept talking to him, telling him help was on the way," Carter recalled.

Paramedics took McDermott to Bert Fish Medical Center, where he woke up four hours later in intensive care. He suffered a concussion, a broken nose, and cuts on his face requiring fifteen stitches, thanks to the tarpon.

Said McDermott, who spent two days in the hospital, "I've been surfing for sixteen years, and I've never heard of anything like this happening. I'm an avid fisherman. Maybe the tarpon was just getting me back for all the tarpon I've caught."

When a father and son caught a monster tiger shark, it triggered a chain of events that led to one of the most bizarre murder mysteries in Australian history.

On April 18, 1935, Bert Hobson and his son Ron, the owners of the Coogee Aquarium in Sydney, netted a six-foot shark that they planned to display in their new shark exhibit. Before they could bring it on board their boat, a monster tiger shark gobbled up the smaller shark and wound up getting caught in their net.

They were thrilled with their unexpected good fortune and brought the tiger shark back to the aquarium and released it in their new shark tank. But the sea creature seemed sick and disoriented.

Three days later, a crowd had gathered at the aquarium to view the latest addition. They oohed and aahed at the size of the tiger shark but then they gasped in horror and disgust when it vomited, expelling the remains of a human arm.

The arm, which had a piece of rope tied around the wrist, sported a faded tattoo of two boxers facing each other with fists raised. Police were immediately called in to investigate. When the tiger shark died five days later, authorities conducted an autopsy, which revealed that the creature had not eaten the arm; it had eaten the smaller shark that had swallowed the arm only a few days earlier.

Police realized they were dealing with a murder and not a shark attack because of one vital piece of evidence: the arm had not been bitten off; it had been cut off with a knife or a scalpel. Investigators worked on the theory that the victim had been slain and his body had been cut up and tossed into the sea, where the perpetrator no doubt hoped sharks would consume the remains.

Not in his worst nightmare could the killer have ever imagined that a tiger shark would be the one to alert police of the murder.

For days, the newspapers ran front-page stories about the shark, the arm, and the murder mystery. Meanwhile, a Sydney woman went to the police, claiming the arm she saw in newspaper photographs belonged to her missing husband, forty-year-old James Smith, a billiards player and bookmaker.

The investigation led police to John Patrick Brady, forty-two, of Sydney, a well-known criminal who had shady dealings with the victim. Authorities discovered that around the time Smith disappeared, Brady had moved out of his cottage, taking with him a tin storage trunk, an anchor, and two heavy window weights.

Brady was arrested and charged with murder. He denied any involvement in the slaying, claiming that he had last seen Smith with Reginald Holmes, a Sydney boat builder for whom Smith had worked before getting fired.

Police went looking for Holmes without success. But then, exactly one month after the shark threw up Smith's arm, investigators got a break. On the night of May 21, police pursued a boat that was operating recklessly in Sydney Harbor. During a tense four-hour chase, the boater attempted to ram his craft into a police launch four times before he was apprehended. The boater was none other than Reginald Holmes, dazed and bleeding from a gunshot wound to his head.

He claimed he had been shot by unknown assailants earlier in the evening and that when the police chased him, he mistakenly assumed they were his attackers. But after police found a .32 caliber pistol in his boat, they suspected Holmes had tried to kill himself but the bullet had only grazed his head.

Under questioning, Holmes told detectives that Brady had murdered Smith, cut him up, stuffed his body in a trunk, and dumped it in the ocean. Holmes further claimed that Brady threatened to kill him if he ratted on Brady. Holmes was not charged on condition that he remain in Sydney and testify at an inquest into Smith's murder.

Holmes never made it to the inquest. On June 11, he was found slumped over the steering wheel of his parked car with three bullets in his head. He had been shot at close range with a .32 caliber pistol. John Brady couldn't have done it because he was in police custody at the time of Holmes's murder.

At the inquest, Holmes's widow, Inie Parker-Holmes, testified that her late husband told her that Brady, whom he knew well, had confessed to him that he killed Smith, placed the cut-up body in a trunk, and dumped it at sea.

The case went to trial, but it was shrouded in allegations and rumors of drug trafficking and organized crime. On the stand, Brady testified that on the night of April 8, he and Smith were together but then Smith had left in the company of two notorious gangsters, Albert Stannard and John Strong.

Brady was acquitted because of insufficient evidence. He changed his name and dropped out of sight. Police continued their investigation and soon charged Stannard and Strong with murder—but of Holmes, not Smith. Like Brady, however, they were acquitted.

To this day, the murder that was first revealed by a tiger shark remains unsolved.

A shark caught off the coast of Jamaica caused a ship to be seized and a captain to be convicted of perjury.

Back in the late 1700s, the harbors of the British West Indies were closed to American ships. But merchants both in the United States and in the islands found the trade too profitable to be given up lightly, so they tried to evade the British navy, which was out to capture any American ship found in the Caribbean.

In 1799, the *Nancy*, a three-masted vessel owned by Baltimore-based merchants, sailed from Maryland to Dutch Curaçao. One of her owners managed to become a naturalized

Dutch citizen on the island, and then assumed command of the ship for her voyage home. He carried two sets of ship's papers—American and Dutch—and intended to produce the Dutch documents if challenged by a British warship.

On its way back, the *Nancy* encountered a terrible storm near Haiti and broke her maintop mast. As she headed toward a small island for repairs, the vessel was chased and captured by the British cutter H.M.S. *Sparrow*, commanded by James Wylie. The *Nancy* was then taken to Kingston, Jamaica, where Captain Wylie brought suit in the Court of Vice Admiralty to condemn the ship and all her merchandise as a lawful prize taken on the high seas.

In court, the *Nancy*'s captain gave his affidavit that his vessel was wrongly held, and produced his papers from Curaçao, which seemed to prove his statement that he and the ship were Dutch.

The case would have been dismissed if it hadn't been for a couple of British sailors who were fishing for shark.

Two days after the capture of the *Nancy*, Lieutenant Michael Fitton, in command of the H.M.S. *Ferret*, a tender of the flagship H.M.S. *Abergavenny*, invited Captain Wylie to breakfast aboard the *Ferret*. While waiting for Wylie to row over from the *Sparrow*, Fitton watched his sailors haul a huge shark onto the deck of the *Ferret*.

When the sailors cut the shark open they discovered the American papers of the *Nancy*, which the captain had thrown overboard when he saw that he could not outrun the *Sparrow*. Fitton was spreading the papers out on the deck as Wylie came aboard. When Wylie read the documents, he immediately rushed them over to the admiralty court before the case could be dismissed. As a result, the *Nancy* and her cargo were condemned as a lawful prize, and her captain was convicted of perjury.

Holy Mackerel!

The documents have forever been known as "the shark papers."

An angler caught a fish that creeped him out, and everyone else who saw it too. That's because it appeared to have a human face.

On May 1, 1929, Julius Gabriel, a shoemaker from Allentown, Pennsylvania, was fishing off a pier at Asbury Park, New Jersey, when he reeled in the fish with a face.

The creature, which witnesses said was either a skate or a ray, had a large, human-looking mouth, eyes set properly with respect to the mouth, and the suggestion of a human-looking nose. A broad flap of heavy flesh gave the appearance of a high forehead. Below the head and neck, the body was similar to that of a human with a well-defined chest and breasts. Like the stingray, it had a long pointed tail with spines along the entire length. The flat underside of the fish was white while the upper side was sand-colored, the protective coloration of fish that feed on the ocean bottom.

Gabriel was so spooked by his eerie catch that he told reporters he didn't plan on fishing for a while. "On the next cast I might catch the devil himself instead of one of his assistants."

A Nebraska couple didn't need bait to attract the fish in their lake. All they had to do was whistle and bang on a dishpan.

In the mid-1920s, Ed Pasco and his wife bought Lake Genevieve, a fishing resort in Freemont, Nebraska. For several years, whenever they threw dead minnows or bits of food into the lake, they whistled and thumped a pan. Eventually, the fish started coming to the dock with just a whistle or a bang from the Pascos. Bluegills, crappies, and bullheads swarmed in by the hundreds.

Unfortunately for fishermen, the anglers weren't allowed to fish near the dock. They had to go out in the lake and use a rod and reel. "It wouldn't be fair to the fish," Pasco told a reporter in 1930. "They trust me and I don't propose to have their confidence abused."

Reel Whoppers

Amazing Fishing Records

WHEN CAPTAIN CORNELIUS CHOY guided his forty-eight-foot charter fishing boat, the *Coreen C*, out of the Honolulu Marina on June 6, 1970, he had onboard three anglers, their wives, and his teenage daughter Gail. They went out hoping to land a marlin. They returned with a world record so big it had to be towed back to port.

Known as "Choy's Monster," the Pacific blue marlin weighed an incredible 1,805 pounds. To this day it's the largest marlin ever taken on rod and reel.

Vacationers Mike Wachtier, Pat Morello, and Charles Lewis had chartered the boat for a day of sportfishing. While off the island of Oahu, Gail Choy-Kaleiki, who was acting as her father's deckhand, yelled, "Marlin!" at the top of her lungs. "We swarmed down to help the client get into the fighting chair, but it was too much fish for him," Choy later told the *New York Daily News*. None of the anglers were experienced, so they passed the rod around during the first hours of the battle with the marlin. Exhausted and sea-sick, they handed the rod off to Gail, who fought the monster while her dad managed the helm. Then father and daughter switched roles.

Like a jet moving over the water, the marlin raced away from the boat time and again. "As I held the rod, I felt it double and the butt kicked me in the belly," Choy recalled. "I came back hard and felt his weight, striking me again and again and again."

With the heavy rod arching and the reel screaming, the marlin leaped clear, glistening a silver blue in the afternoon sun. "As he hit the water he threw a column of spray like a bomb bursting," said Choy. "Then he came out again and the spray roared. The line felt slack for a second and then he burst out. He headed across and wildly jumped twice more, hanging high and stiff in the air.

"I could see the hook in the corner of his mouth. Unless a marlin is hooked where it hurts, he makes his fight not against the pain from the hook but against being captured.

That's what this old blue marlin did. He took off like a grey-hound in a series of jumps."

The fish jumped forty-two times to the southeast during a struggle that lasted eight hours. "Every time he jumped it was a sight to make your heart stand still," said the captain.

Meanwhile, Gail, who was at the helm part of the time, followed the fish with the boat as Choy remained standing. The line was taut as a banjo string and sweat was pouring down his face until finally he had a straight pull out toward the fish. Choy pulled the fish up quickly before the sharks got to it and then Gail wired it. Because of the fish's size, they had to tow it into port.

"That fish was the king of the marlins," said Gail.

Naturally, it could not qualify for an IGFA world record because more than one angler was involved in landing the monster. But the marlin, which was mounted in the

International Market on Waikiki, is still the largest blue ever taken on rod and reel.

Added Choy, "There is great pleasure in being on the sea in the unknown wild suddenness of a great fish in his life-and-death struggle while your strength is harnessed to his; and there is satisfaction in conquering this thing that rules the sea."

Catching and officially weighing a two-hundred-pound tarpon has been an elusive dream of fly fishermen. Only one man has actually lived that dream—Jim Holland, Jr.

Holland, a twenty-four-year-old law student from Vancouver, Washington, made fly-fishing history on May 11, 2001, when he landed a 202 ½-pound tarpon while fishing the flats near Homosassa, Florida. He boated the record catch after a two-hour battle on twenty-pound test tippet and a "slick slider" fly. During the fight, the boat he was in chased the fish for more than three miles and warded off a bull shark.

The IGFA certified the fish, topping the previous record of 188 pounds caught in the same area in 1983 by fly-fishing expert Billy Pate, Jr.

Holland and his father James Senior were enjoying their last day of a week-long fishing trip in the area with local guide Captain Steve Kilpatrick on his sixteen-foot Silver King skiff, *Kasea*.

Holland hooked the fish from a school of large silver kings that approached the boat in a tarpon hot spot on Florida's west coast. "Because of the poor visibility, I aimed for the first big black back that I saw and fired at it," he said in *Saltwater Flyfishing* magazine. "Luckily, my shot flew true, and landed right on target."

He said the next thirty seconds was a blur as the fish launched halfway out of the water twice directly away from the boat, but he had no idea that he had a record on the other end of the line. Although they knew it looked big, they couldn't see its girth, so they couldn't accurately gauge exactly how big it was. "This is perhaps the greatest piece of luck of all," he said. "Not knowing the size of the fish enabled me to remain calm, settle into a good fighting rhythm, and pressure the tarpon as hard as I would any other without worrying about losing a world record."

Holland caught the fish on a tarpon streamer tied the night before by Kilpatrick. The fly was a black, white, and red deer-hair slider, tied on a size 5/0 Owner hook.

The captain used the electric trolling motor to chase the fish three miles over the flats, then spotted a big bull shark angling toward their prize. "I started up the gasoline motor and kept revving it up, using the sound to disturb the shark's sensory system," Kilpatrick said.

When the worn-out tarpon came alongside, Kilpatrick had his first clue to how large it was. "When I used a lip gaff and went to lift the fish, I couldn't even budge it," said the six-foot, three-inch, 230-pound captain.

Once the anglers brought the tarpon onto the deck, "we knew this was a special fish," said Holland. "When Dad ran his calculations based on the length and girth method and it came up 206 pounds, we were all stunned. We're strictly catch and release anglers, so killing this beautiful creature hadn't even entered my mind until that very moment.

Realizing the significance of the event, we really had no choice."

After landing the fish, Holland, his father, and Kilpatrick sped back to the dock to find a certified scale on which to weigh the tarpon. Grabbing a scale from the back of a fellow guide's pickup, the group headed to Kilpatrick's tarpon camp and suspended the seven-foot fish so that its weight could be accurately gauged.

Holland said that when he looked at the scale, he shouted, "Oh my God, we just made history!"

While the fifty-one-foot Bertram *Lucky II* was on its first fishing trip, one of its anglers caught the largest blue marlin in the history of the Gulf of Mexico.

Conrad Hawkins, of Jacksonville, Florida, landed a record-setting 1,046-pound blue marlin during the Bay Point Invitational Billfish Tournament out of Panama City on July 14, 2001. The new boat was about seventy miles offshore in 110 fathoms when the fish inhaled a large plastic lure running from the starboard outrigger. Hawkins jumped in the fighting chair and set the hook hard.

Although Captain Tommy Browning immediately reversed the boat, the marlin took about 750 yards of the thousand-yard spool of hundred-pound line. Hawkins fought the fish for almost three hours, cranking it toward the boat seven times, but each time the marlin broke loose from the mate's grip on the six hundred-pound test Jinkai steel leader and made another long run. While Hawkins was winching the marlin to the boat for the fourth time, the harness strapped to the fighting chair snapped from the strain, but the crew jury-rigged another harness.

Finally, after the eighth run, the crew gaffed and roped the prize, but it was too heavy to lift into the boat. Captain Browning turned downsea and used the waves to help shove the fish aboard.

"She came up out of the water and we saw the whole bill and her head, and everybody started screaming," Hawkins recalled. "The captain said he'd been out there forty years and never seen a fish that big.

"We'd count to three and move her four inches at a time. When we finally got her in, her head was at the cabin and her tail was still hanging out the door. We had to remove the fighting chair."

With the marlin's tail hanging off the stern, the *Lucky II* raced back to Panama City. Bags of ice were packed around the fish to lessen weight loss, and a tarpaulin was placed over it. Meanwhile, word of the catch was spreading, and thousands gathered at the Bay Point Marina dock. "Boats loaded with people started coming out to greet us, helicopters were coming over, and TV people were taking pictures—it was an amazing event," Hawkins said.

After the *Lucky II* pulled into the harbor, it took a fourteen-man deck crew to string the monster upside down only to discover that the fish was too heavy for the thousand-pound scale. Fortunately, Nathan Miller, owner of a metals recycling business, was in the crowd and offered to let them use the certified scale at his warehouse thirteen miles away.

So Hawkins's marlin was muscled into a refrigerated truck and escorted by a police cruiser, its lights flashing all the way, to the warehouse. "We didn't stop for anything—red lights, nothing," said Hawkins, who rode in the police car.

This time, it took sixteen men, eight on a side, to carry the marlin onto a pallet and then onto the digital scale. With an IGFA official looking on, the weight was recorded at 1,046 pounds. That easily surpassed the Florida record by 66 pounds and beat the Gulf of Mexico mark of 1,018, which is the Louisiana record. The marlin measured 131 inches and had a girth of 78 inches.

"It's mind-boggling how big this fish was," Hawkins said. "It really dawns on you when you think of the thousands and thousands of boats that have fished for this thing.

"It was an unbelievable lifetime event."

The freshwater world record that has stood the longest is, ironically, for one of the most frequently caught fish—the yellow perch.

Dr. C. C. Abbot landed a four-pound, three-ounce yellow perch in the Delaware River near Bordentown, New Jersey, in May 1865, according to the IGFA. Despite the millions of perch that have been caught since, Abbot's record still stands as the largest perch ever reeled in as of 2003.

Several other freshwater records set between World War I and the Depression have yet to be topped. Among them:

- A fourteen-pound, eight-ounce brook trout caught by Dr. W. T. Cook on the Nipigon River in Ontario, July 1916.

- A fifty-one-pound, three-ounce tiger muskel-lunge caught by John Knobla on Lac Vieux-Desert between Wisconsin and Michigan, July 16, 1919.

- A forty-one-pound cutthroat trout caught by John Skimmerhorn on Pyramid Lake, Nevada, December 1925.

- A seventy-nine-pound, two-ounce Atlantic salmon caught by Henrik Henriksen in the Tana River, Norway, 1928.

When George Perry went fishing on June 2, 1932, he had no idea he would set a world record for largemouth bass that, as of 2003, has remained unequaled for more than seventy years and has become the most coveted of all freshwater fishing marks.

The bass meant more to Perry as food than as a seminal moment in angling. Back then, all the twenty-year-old farm boy cared about was helping to provide for his family. It was the height of the Great Depression, and his father had died the year before. Perry, who had only an eighth grade education, was the main provider for his mother, two brothers, and two sisters. He caught fish and shot deer and squirrels for the dinner table.

On that memorable day, he and one of his brothers went out on Montgomery Lake deep in a cypress swamp in south-central Georgia. They had to share the rod and reel, which cost $1.33, and had only one lure worth $1.35. They fished with twenty-five-pound test waterproof silk line from a rowboat built from seventy-five cents' worth of second-hand lumber scraps.

"We were out to catch dinner," he recalled years later. "I tossed the lure back into a pocket between two fallen trees and gave the plug a couple of jerks. All at once, the water splashed everywhere. I do remember striking, then raring back and trying to reel. But nothing budged. I thought I'd lost the fish—that it had dived and hung me up. What had me really worried was the [possibility of losing the] lure because it was the only one we had between us."

But eventually Perry reeled in the bass without too much of a fight. After the fish was landed, Perry toted it over to the J. J. Hall and Co. general store in nearby Helena, where he lived. In a *Sports Afield* article, Perry said, "It was almost an accident that I had the fish weighed and recorded." A buddy mentioned that *Field & Stream* was running a contest that offered $75 in merchandise to the angler who caught the biggest largemouth bass that year. So Perry took his fish to the post office where, several hours after it was caught, the big female weighed in at twenty-two pounds, four ounces and measured thirty-one inches long and twenty-seven inches around.

"It created a lot of attention that day in Helena," said Perry. "The old fellow in the general store was also a notary public and made the whole thing official."

Perry brought his fish home where his mother Laura filleted it and fried one side for supper, along with onions and tomatoes from the garden. They ate the other fillet later. Perry won the *Field & Stream* contest, earning him a Browning automatic shotgun, a rod and reel, shotgun shells, and some outdoor clothing. At the time, this seemed to Perry like all the gear in the world.

Nobody took a photo, but the family does have a replica of the record bass and the lure Perry used.

According to Bill Baab, who knew Perry and wrote an article about him in the February 1989 issue of *Bassin'*, the lure was a #241 jointed perch Wiggle Fish manufactured by the Creek Chub Bait Co. But the makers of the line, rod, and reel used by Perry remain unknown.

Perry never seemed very impressed with his record. Baab said the angler was "a quiet but confident man" who educated himself and became an industrious self-made man. He eventually learned to fly and owned Perry's Flying Service in Brunswick, Georgia. He died in a plane crash in 1974.

Today there is a historical marker on the side of Georgia Route 117 about 2 ½ miles from Montgomery Lake commemorating Perry's record.

While the legendary catch was born of the search for dinner, anglers the world over are hoping to top that mark not only for the fame but for the money from sponsorships, clinics, promotions, endorsements, and ad revenues. Shortly before his death in 2000, Bob Kutz, director of the National Freshwater Fishing Hall of Fame, noted, "The next world-record largemouth bass, if it ever comes, will be worth a million dollars. Prizes, endorsements, outdoor shows; it could be incredible."

Perry might not have understood that. Like many people who were brought up in the Depression, he knew what was really important in life. Said Dr. William F. Austin, of Brunswick, an old friend of Perry's, "He was never very impressed by the fish, or interested in impressing anyone about it."

On August 3, 2001, Charles Ashley, Jr., caught a 116-pound, 12-ounce blue catfish that set a new all-tackle world record.

No one in the catfishing community was surprised to hear the record came from the Mississippi River, but most were amazed that it was caught on a hundred-degree summer afternoon on tackle better suited for bullhead fishing—and, most surprising of all, with a chunk of Spam for bait.

Yes, the same processed pork product that fed Allied soldiers throughout World War II helped land a world record.

Ashley, twenty-four, of Marion, Arkansas, was catfishing with two friends on the Arkansas side of the Mississippi River in West Memphis just south of the Interstate 55 bridge. He was using an inexpensive medium-weight spinning combo he had recently bought and a reel spooled with twenty-pound test line. After he baited the hook with a chunk of Spam, he cast it out and let it sink to the bottom.

"We've used Spam a long time for catfish," he told the *Morning News*. "It's our favorite bait. My daddy used it and my granddaddy too." He said his five-year-old son was learning to fish and also becoming a Spam fan. "We just cut it in chunks and run one of them on a single hook, not a treble hook. It's good catfish bait."

Anchored off a rock dike in a fourteen-foot flat-bottom aluminum boat, Ashley had fished for thirty minutes without a bite. Then his line began moving off. "I knew it was a good fish after I set the hook. The biggest catfish I had caught before was about twenty pounds and I thought this one would be that big.

"The fish just pulled away from us. It never did go down deep. But every time it decided to move off, it peeled the drag. When we finally got the fish to roll up at the surface, we forgot about the dip net. No way would its head go in the net." Instead when the fish was exhausted after a forty-five-minute battle, Ashley put down his rod and wrestled the fish into the boat.

He took it to the fish market and called the Arkansas Game and Fish Commission. Wildlife officer Kirk Harris witnessed the weighing of the huge catfish on certified scales. It measured sixty-two inches long and 38½ inches in girth.

"That was the first time I had used the outfit, and this was the first fish I caught on it," said Ashley. And it's the first time that Spam was used for bait to land a world record.

Adrian Molloy believed he would one day catch a record bluefin tuna off the coast of Ireland with rod and reel. Few believed him, especially after he failed in his quest year after year.

"For years these same people laughed at me for dreaming it was possible, but they're not laughing now," said Molloy, after reeling in a European record 968-pound tuna.

On October 14, 2001, Molloy, of Kilcar, Donegal, Ireland, and his friend Michael Callaghan, of nearby Killybegs, headed out along the Donegal County coast in their twenty-two-foot boat. For five years Molloy had dreams of landing a big tuna, but he always had returned from his fishing trip without such a prize catch. This fall morning looked like it would be another disappointment. Neither angler had so much as a nibble for several hours as they tailed a school of tuna.

"Suddenly we saw one of the fish had turned to follow us and was a few hundred yards behind," Molloy told the *Daily Mail*. "We saw him mouth at the lure before he took it. We knew he was a good one because he took out an unbelievable amount of line in seconds. The line was screaming like I had never heard before. Until you have seen a fish like that on the line, you can't grasp how much pressure they put on it."

The tuna raced three hundred yards away once it was hooked and battled for an hour and forty minutes before giving up. Molloy used an American Penn rod with an artificial lure and 130-pound class tackle.

"It was an inch-by-inch battle," he said. "I could only reel in when he stopped running, and even then it was a mighty struggle to haul him in. The fish fought unbelievably hard until we got it alongside the boat and we managed to secure its tail."

When Molloy triumphantly returned to the docks, he recalled, "people were amazed at the size of the beast. Everybody was wondering who could have caught such a fish from such a small boat."

A representative from the food company John West estimated the tuna would provide enough meat to fill 2,402 cans or make 6,846 sandwiches.

Molloy said there are even bigger fish waiting to be caught off the Irish coast. "This could be the start of big-game fishing in Ireland," he said.

Perhaps he's right. But anglers around the Emerald Isle face a mighty big challenge to break the bluefin tuna world record of 1,496 pounds, which was caught off Nova Scotia in 1979.

Amanda Broadbent wasn't too keen on going on her first fishing trip with her husband Rick to celebrate their first wedding anniversary, but she went along anyway. She was glad she did. The reluctant angler caught a catfish that topped the world record by about ten pounds.

In June 2002, the Broadbents, from Greater Manchester, England, went on a fishing trip to the River Ebro in eastern Spain. It was the first time she had accompanied her husband, who had gone fishing there with friends annually for years.

"Fishing isn't really my thing," Amanda told the BBC. "I only wanted to get some sun. I just went along in the boat to keep Rick company and thought I'd have a go at fishing."

Two days into their vacation, Amanda cast her line and ended up battling an enormous catfish. Rick had to grab his wife by her shorts to stop her from being pulled into the river. Their boat spun around on its anchor as the fish—which Amanda said looked like the Loch Ness Monster—fought hard.

Reel Whoppers

When she brought the fish to the boat, the fishing rod snapped. But Rick and their guide leaned over the boat and hauled it in. "Rick couldn't believe his eyes," she said. "I think he was a bit jealous."

The fish measured six feet long—ten inches more than Amanda—and weighed 126 pounds. After taking photos of it with her, they threw it back into the river, giving up the chance to verify a world record.

Armed only with a mask, a spear, fins, and the air in their lungs, breath-hold divers venture into the open ocean to track and catch fish, which sometimes are twice the diver's size. Or in Donald Pinder's case, four times the size.

On May 10, 1949, Pinder was free diving off the coast of Miami when he encountered an 804-pound jewfish.

He successfully speared it, setting a world record that still stands today, according to the International Underwater Spearfishing Association. The old record was held by his brother Art, who achieved fame as a world-class spearfisherman by snaring a seven-and-one-half-foot sailfish and a 337-pound tiger shark.

Art was bitten by sharks four times. Once while he was lobster diving, a nurse shark clamped onto his left arm and didn't let go until Art reached the surface and his wife Alice, who was in their boat, hit the shark in the head with a hammer. As she pleaded with Art to get back in the boat, he patted the loose skin back into place and went down to get the lobster that would be that night's dinner. He later duct-taped the skin back to his arm.

Art, Donald, and their brother Fred became legendary figures in spearfishing. Using pole spears and homemade copper goggles, the early spearfishermen stalked their prey without the benefit of scuba tanks. These free divers went after shark, tuna, and other big fish, while holding their breath for well over two minutes at a time.

The brothers' weapon was a Hawaiian sling, which consisted of a handheld piece of wood, surgical tubing, and a five-foot steel rod. Few had more success with the Hawaiian sling, which was shot like a bow and arrow, than the Pinder brothers, who teamed to win a national spearfishing championship in 1954.

A shark angler who was determined to land a world record achieved his goal and more—because he reeled in the largest fish that was ever caught and certified.

Australian Alf Dean had racked up several of his country's sharkfishing records, but he wasn't satisfied. He wanted to be the first to bring in a game fish weighing more than one ton.

In the wee hours of the morning of April 21, 1959, Dean and his skipper, Ken Puckridge, were chumming for shark in Streaky Bay off South Australia. Suddenly at about 3:30 A.M., they felt a bump that almost caused them to lose their balance. A tremendously large shark had hit their boat. In the brief glimpse he had of the beast in the boat's floodlights, Dean knew this was a great white big enough to be a world record. But he wasn't about to fight it in the dark, so he kept teasing the shark with chum, keeping it interested until the first light of dawn.

Once he hooked the great white on thirty-nine-gauge thread line, it took Dean only forty-eight minutes to muscle it to the boat. During the battle, the shark charged the boat and tried to bite the propeller and hull. It leaped twice out of the water toward the vessel.

"We were able to work the fish all the time without much line out," Dean told reporters later. "The fight wasn't that hard. I did worry a bit when the fish jumped. It's something to see such a big fish slam back into the water after jumping clear."

After the shark was gaffed and tail-roped, Dean and Puckridge returned to a mob scene at the weighing station. The shark measured sixteen feet, ten inches and was more than nine feet in girth; it weighed a whopping 2,664 pounds.

It was the first game fish weighing more than one ton ever landed by rod and reel anywhere in the world, according to the South Australian Big Game Fishermen's Association. Larger sharks have been caught on rod and reel but they were landed on line heavier than the IGFA maximum 130-pound test or were using the wrong bait.

The largest sea creature ever caught on rod and reel was the 3,427-pound, sixteen-foot, eight-inch great white shark caught on August 6, 1986, by two charter boat captains, Frank Mundus and Donnie Braddick, about forty miles offshore of Montauk, Long Island.

Braddick was the angler in the chair, while Mundus baited the shark, ran the boat, and supervised the kill. (Mundus, by the way, was the inspiration for the character Quint, the crusty professional shark hunter, in the movie *Jaws*.)

The day before the catch, Braddick had spotted a dead whale floating in the ocean and knew it would lead to a shark feast. That night, after dropping off their fishing parties at port, Braddick, Mundus, and mate Joe DiLeonardo returned to the whale.

By noon the next day, six great whites were circling around the area. DiLeonardo was in the chair for the hookup of an estimated two thoussand-pounder, but twenty minutes later, it was gone. The ⅛-inch stainless-steel cable leader, on which cutting pliers are useless, had been bitten in two.

Mundus enticed another, even bigger, great white by offering the bait, but withdrawing it as soon as the shark showed interest. Soon the shark was more interested in Mundus's bait than the whale. This time, Braddick was in the chair for the hookup at about 4:30 P.M.

"It felt like a freight train," Braddick recalled. "The first time he came up he thrashed around only about twenty-five feet from the boat. The second time he started about fifty feet behind the boat and came right at us. The third time he was rolled up in the leader and way out of the water with his pecs spread, flapping his jaws in slow motion. It was awesome. My line was actually going up."

He fought the shark for about two hours before DiLeonardo got a gaff into it, then another gaff before using a head choker and tail rope.

The great white was brought back to the docks at Montauk to a carnival atmosphere as hundreds of fishermen and curiosity seekers whooped and hollered. The shark was so heavy that an inch-thick rope being used to hoist the fish broke.

"I've always wanted to catch a world-record great white," Braddick said.

Unfortunately, his record catch officially remains unofficial. Because of questions concerning the bait and the line test, the IGFA refused to recognize it.

Fishing Trip-Ups

Crazy Mishaps While Fishing

A GIANT SWORDFISH hooked off the Mexican coast jumped into a fisherman's boat and stabbed the man through his abdomen.

On March 27, 2001, angler Jose Rojas Mayarita, thirty-nine, was alone on his boat off the coast of Acapulco when he hooked a ten-foot swordfish. As Jose was reeling it in, the fish leaped out of the water and landed on him. The marlin's spear pierced the fisherman's stomach and came out the other side. Somehow he was able to pull out the spear after the fish had died, but he was too weak to do anything else. He drifted in his boat for two days before anglers from another vessel spotted him and rescued him.

Jose was taken to the General Hospital in Acapulco where he was treated and released days later.

A year later another swordfish severely injured a fisherman off the coast of southern India.

According to Press Trust of India, angler Nicholas Mani was relaxing in his boat when the swordfish jumped from the water and landed on him so fiercely that its bill struck him in the left eye and became embedded.

Mani was taken to the Aravind Eye Hospital in Madurai where doctors removed the swordfish's bill from the fisherman's eye after an hour-long operation. It was not known if the sight in his injured eye could be restored.

In the span of just a few days in August 2002, four anglers in north Florida were clobbered by flying sturgeon.

The federally protected fish can grow more than nine feet long and weigh more than three hundred pounds. Sturgeon, which have rows of bony plates that line their body like alligators, have been listed as threatened since 1991, so no one is allowed to catch and keep them.

Brian Clemens, fifty, of Panama City, Florida, was struck by a sturgeon while he was fishing on the Choctawhatchee River. "We hit head-on," he told the *Miami Herald*. "I didn't have time to duck, dodge, or do anything. It splattered me."

He suffered a cracked sternum, two broken ribs, and a collapsed lung and needed sixteen stitches.

Just days earlier, another fisherman and his girlfriend were slammed overboard by one of the leaping fish on the Suwannee River. Not only that but a female angler was knocked unconscious and suffered three broken ribs and a collapsed lung after a flying sturgeon bashed into her on the same river.

The Florida Fish and Wildlife Conservation Commission and U.S. Fish and Wildlife Service received dozens of calls from fishermen wondering why the sturgeon appeared to be launching unprovoked attacks on anglers.

Said USFWS biologist Patty Kelly, "We had calls asking, 'Are they attacking people on purpose?' That's ridiculous. It's a purely random act. Sturgeon have no teeth. They're very docile. They don't try to bite you. They just try to get away."

Fishing Trip-Ups

She said that the sturgeon collisions happened because "there are more people using the rivers."

On a summer day in 2002, Thai fisherman Tongsuk Kungked caught a small fish on the bank of a river. Because he wanted his hands free to hold his fishing rod and rebait the line, he put the squirming fish in his mouth. That was a big mistake.

The live fish began wiggling and pushed its way further into his mouth until it got jammed in his throat. No matter how hard he tried, Tongsuk couldn't yank the fish out. But at least he was able to breathe, although not very well.

He managed to get home and have his wife rush him to Prasat Hospital in Surin, where a doctor had to cut open Tongsuk's throat to remove the fish. The twenty-six-year-old angler told the newspaper *Kao Sod* that he was in extreme pain when he swallowed the fish.

At least Tongsuk lived to tell the tale. According to the syndicated newspaper column "Earthweek," a sleepy Brazilian fisherman on the Maguari River in the Amazon choked to death on a fish that jumped into his mouth in 1996. While Nathon do Nascimento yawned in his boat, a six-inch fish leaped out of the water and became lodged in his throat. Although his fishing buddies tried to get him medical assistance, he didn't make it to the hospital in time.

Fishing Trip-Ups

Two years later, Harris Simbawa, twenty-eight, caught a fish on the banks of the Chengu River, near Livingstone, Zambia, and tried to bite off its head. That was the local method used to kill fish. But the catch slipped down his throat, choking him to death. Villagers found his body with a stick dangling from his mouth. He had apparently tried to dislodge the fish with the stick, but had only pushed it farther down his gullet.

Richard Burkle's big fish got away—but not before he was shot. The fisherman, not the fish.

On August 12, 1961, Burkle went fishing near the Seven Mile Bridge close to Marathon, Florida. Standing on an embankment, he hooked a shark—a big one. Because he was having a difficult time landing it, he pulled out a pistol to finish off the shark.

A split second before Burkle fired, the shark jerked hard on the line, causing the angler to lose his balance. The bullet missed its mark, but found another—Burkle's left leg. He crawled to the highway nearby, where he managed to get into his car and drive to a state police station. Police then rushed him to Baptist Hospital in Miami, where the bullet was removed.

As for the shark, Burkle told reporters, "I forgot all about him. I guess he still has my hook in his mouth."

Two fishermen caught in a storm off the Bahamas wound up losing their boat and drifting for thirty-one agonizing hours in shark-infested waters—in fiberglass beer coolers.

Fishing Trip-Ups

The ordeal for Robert Rice, thirty-seven, and David Federico, twenty-six, began on the morning of September 16, 1979, when they set out in their twenty-three-foot fishing boat from Palm Beach, Florida, for West End in the Bahamas, about sixty miles away.

About fifteen miles from their destination, disaster struck. Their powerboat split open in ten-foot seas and within four minutes sank like a rock in three thousand feet of water. The anglers managed to salvage their life preservers, rope, three cans of beer, and two fiberglass coolers— each large enough to hold a person. They tied the coolers together and hopped in.

"Gasoline was thick all around us," Rice later told reporters. "My skin felt like it was on fire. Waves were washing over me, and I was gagging on seawater. Every few minutes a wave curled over us and flipped us upside down. I thought about how our boat disappeared without a trace and how we could disappear just as fast."

After dark, the jellyfish began to sting them. By morning, their arms and hands were raw and red from the stings. "And as we drank our first beer, I began to worry about sharks. Suddenly, in the distance I spotted a fin slicing through the water straight for us. About ten feet away, it dove and then . . . wham! It hit my cooler and knocked me out of it. My arms and legs turned into propellers. I hardly touched the water before I scrambled back into the cooler." Fortunately, the shark didn't return.

Later that afternoon, crewmen aboard the Japanese freighter *Seki Rokako* spotted the hapless fishermen and rescued them.

On October 16, 1963, William Cheatham was surf fishing on the beach of Panama City, Florida, when a strong strike bent his pole, so he waded out about thirty feet in the clear, four-foot-deep water. He never would've stepped out that far had he known what lurked behind him.

According to the *Panama City News-Herald*, the angler lost his fish and a moment later felt something bump his right leg. He turned around and looked with alarm at a five-hundred-pound shark that had targeted him for its next meal. After two menacing passes at him, the shark struck, viciously ripping into the calf of his right leg and knocking him down.

Bleeding badly, Cheatham tried to stand up, but the shark rammed him again, causing him to slip under the water. As the shark came in for the kill, the wounded fisherman managed to shove the creature while avoiding its mouth. Then he grabbed the shark's body behind its pectoral fin and rode the giant fish for several seconds until he slipped off. The shark swam away as Cheatham limped to the beach and collapsed in the sand. Passersby transported him to the hospital, where doctors treated his mauled right calf and foot.

Fishing Trip-Ups

Neither wind nor snow nor crack of ice deterred hundreds of ice fishermen—even when they became stranded after a frozen lake cracked.

On the weekend of January 25–26, 1997, more than four hundred people were ice fishing in a derby on Lake Simcoe, the most heavily ice-fished lake in the world. Located about sixty miles from Toronto, the lake had held upward of ten thousand huts at one time.

But the weather was horrible for the derby. Blinding snow and winds of fifty-five miles per hour battered the ice huts. Even worse, the elements combined to cause a crack about ten miles long across the lake, opening a gap from 30 to 110 yards wide between the fishermen and the shore.

The Canadian Forces and three police agencies sent in helicopters, boats, and emergency crews to rescue the stranded anglers. But when the weather deteriorated, the rescue mission was halted. More than two hundred fishermen remained trapped overnight and took shelter in their fishing huts. Provincial police said there were no reports of anyone falling into the water, although a few people suffered mild hypothermia.

What was most amazing to the rescuers was seeing more than a hundred other ice fishermen heading back onto the frozen lake to fish during the rescue mission. Said a headline in the *Toronto Star:* TOUGH TO LEGISLATE COMMON SENSE FOR ICE FISHERMEN. The rescue operation cost Canadian taxpayers nearly $300,000.

Sometimes you just have to let the big one get away. Tragically, Franc Filipic didn't, and it cost him his life.

Fishing Trip-Ups

According to the state-run news agency STA, on August 25, 1998, Filipic, forty-seven, of Ljubljana, Slovenia, was fishing on the banks of a lake in eastern Slovenia when he hooked a large sheatfish, a kind of cat-fish. Determined to land the fish, he walked into the lake while trying to reel it in. The fish—estimated by Filipic's buddy, who witnessed the struggle, to be about six feet long and 110 pounds—dragged the angler into deeper water.

Filipic's friend shouted at him to let go of the rod, but the fisherman refused even after he was pulled under the water. Unfortunately, Filipic never surfaced. Police and divers found the angler's body after a two-day search. The fish and the angler's rod had disappeared.

According to his friend, Filipic's last words were "Now I've got him!"

No one knew what happened to Kang Suk Lee after his fellow fishermen watched him get washed off the rocks in Port Kembla, Australia, on April 2, 2002. The answer was found in the belly of a ten-foot, 815-pound tiger shark nearly three weeks later.

Lee, fifty-two, a Korean immigrant who worked in Sydney as a welder, went fishing at a popular spot near Honeycomb Rocks known as Hill 60. According to a statement given by police at an inquest later, witnesses said Lee was fishing "in a dangerous position where every time a wave would break on the rocks the fisherman would run away from the oncoming wave and return to fishing." But one wave caught Lee and carried him into the surf. Although other anglers tossed him a life preserver, Lee couldn't reach it and was swept away. A large air and sea search failed to find any trace of him.

Nineteen days after Lee's disappearance, angler Robert Brown, of Belmont, Australia, was fishing with three mates on board the *Grumpy I* about sixty miles north of Sydney when he snared a monster shark. But it wasn't until the shark's stomach was slit later that night that its gruesome contents were revealed. The fishermen discovered a human skull, arm, shoulder, and pelvis inside. Dental records revealed that the remains belonged to Lee.

Authorities believed that Lee was already dead when he was consumed by the giant tiger shark. "When recovered from within the shark, the remains did not permit any definitive conclusion to be reached as to whether he had drowned or whether he may have been killed when he was smashed against the rocks by wave action," Senior Police Sergeant Phil Lloyd said in assisting the coroner.

Almost two years earlier, on August 28, 2000, workers at an Australian seafood processing plant made a ghastly discovery when they cut open the stomach of a giant cod—a human head.

Peter Monson, coowner of the A Fine Kettle o' Fish factory in Cairns, said the head was "wholly intact" inside the ninety-eight-pound Morgan cod, which was being filleted and readied for sale.

"It's not an everyday occurrence that you make a discovery like this," Monson told reporters. "There was just total disbelief."

The six-foot fish, which had been caught by a local trawler, was taken away in a body bag for investigation. Reports indicated that the head inside the cod was probably that of fisherman Michael Peter Edwards, who disappeared in the ocean after falling off a trawler near Townsville the previous day.

Bennie Shipp and his wife Vivian were fishing from their trolling motorboat on November 18, 1963, when suddenly Vivian slipped and plunged into the ice-cold water of Chickamauga Lake, Tennessee.

Bennie jumped in after her and grabbed his struggling wife under the shoulders and started to swim back to the boat—except it wasn't there. In his haste to save his wife, Bennie had forgotten to turn off the motor. The boat was moving away from them.

"When we saw that boat leave us in the freezing water, we thought for sure we were goners," recalled Bennie.

Suffering from hypothermia, the couple was nearly unconscious when to their happy surprise the boat made a complete circle and headed back toward them. It came close enough so that Bennie could grab it and climb back in. Then he stopped the engine and plucked his wife out of the water.

"We were lucky," said Bennie. "If the boat had passed one foot farther out, I wouldn't have caught it . . . and we wouldn't have made it."

When a six-foot-long shark got trapped in prawn nets and was hauled aboard a trawler off the coast of Darwin, Australia, May 6, 2002, fisherman Richard Morris tried to throw it back into the sea. That's when the shark caught him.

It clamped its powerful jaws around his arms. Three other crew members rushed to the aid of the twenty-year-old and pried open the shark's jaw by jamming screwdrivers in its mouth. Morris was soon airlifted to Royal Darwin Hospital, where he was treated for severe lacerations.

"We had caught the shark in our prawn nets," recalled trawler skipper John Correria. "We were going to throw it overboard, and Richard went to the head while I picked up the tail. The next thing I knew, I heard him yell. In eleven years at sea I haven't seen anything so awful."

Two men were fishing from their sixteen-foot boat off the coast of New Smyrna Beach, Florida, on February 9, 1999, when suddenly a powerful sea creature somehow got tangled up in the anchor line and began pulling the craft out toward deeper water.

The fishermen put their ninety-horsepower engine in reverse in a frantic effort to stop themselves from being dragged out to sea, but it was no use. So they sent out a radio distress call.

The Coast Guard sent a rescue boat to investigate and found the boat being dragged in circles by something below the Atlantic. The crew transferred the anchor line to the forty-one-foot-long Coast Guard vessel, freeing the fishermen's boat. After the Coast Guard boat pulled on the anchor line for several minutes, a giant manta ray measuring eighteen feet in width and weighing at least three hundred pounds came to the surface. Eventually, following a little tussle, the manta ray freed itself and swam away.

Fishing Trip-Ups

Petty Officer Scott Barnes said the manta ray could have pulled the boat to the bottom if the water had been deep enough. While manta rays have been known to weigh up to three thousand pounds, they usually are much smaller. "If there were just a ledge below and he decided to head down, that boat could have been gone," Barnes said. "Overall, the manta ray pulled their boat for almost two hours and towed it approximately one and a half miles offshore."

While fishing in a quiet pond, two Dutch anglers had a blast—literally.

A German mine had blown up after lying unnoticed in the water since World War II. It happened on an otherwise peaceful May afternoon in 2002 near Enschede, The Netherlands.

Joost Westdorp and Sjuul Eerdmans, who were unharmed, told authorities that the explosion caused the water to shoot up three hundred feet in the air and shower them with dead fish. The banks of the pond were left littered with bits of carp, perch, and pike.

Army bomb disposal experts who investigated the blast said the German mine had about ten pounds of explosives. They believe that a metal shield over the explosives had rusted through, causing the mine to blow up.

On his way to work, Steve Wagner was struck with a severe case of fishing fever. As it turned out, he should have taken an antidote.

Fishing Trip-Ups

Seeing he had ten minutes to spare on the morning of May 30, 2003, Wagner, forty-seven, of Medford, Oregon, decided to stop by the Savage Rapids Dam on the Rogue River to see how the fish were biting. He got out of his car, a 2002 Kia Sportage, and moments later, it was rolling downhill.

Wagner tried to stop the vehicle. First, he got in front of it, but he had no traction because of the steep slope and the slippery gravel that allowed the Kia to keep shoving him downhill. Next, he jumped partway into the moving car, but, hanging half in and half out, he was unable to apply the brake. Finally, he bailed out.

"I rolled onto the hill and then started yelling, 'Heads up! Car coming!' to the people down below," Wagner told the Associated Press. Luckily for the anglers downhill from the driverless Kia, the vehicle careened into a tree and bounced off, which diverted its path away from them but straight into the river.

Within seconds, the sport utility vehicle—with Wagner's wallet, cell phone, digital camera, and tackle—sank in about twenty feet of water on the lakeside of the dam wall.

Authorities, with the help of the Jackson County Dive Team, managed to attach tow cables to the Kia and drag it to the surface with all of Wagner's fishing tackle bobbing inside. Eventually, the car was hauled onto dry land.

Sporting a few scrapes and bruises, a dejected Wagner told a reporter at the scene, "I'll be in the book of dummies for eternity. My wife is definitely going to rescind my fishing privileges."

Two men went fishing for trout and caught more grief than
fish.

In 1986, John Butler (a pseudonym given for reasons
that will soon appear obvious) and his partner were fishing
along California's Convict Creek southeast of Yosemite
National Park. They were boulder hopping, stream jumping,
and shrub ducking for about three hours, and came away
with several rainbows and two German browns.

As they headed home to Orange County in their truck
on U.S. Highway 395, their real troubles began. Here is
Butler's account on fishingnetwork.net (edited, with permission, for brevity) of what happened next:

> After about 15 minutes on the road, my partner said,
> "Well, would you look at that? A damn tick!" I looked
> at his forearm and saw a little red deer tick. He was try-
> ing to be cool, but his voice started to increase in pitch

when he said, "Get it off of me, would you?" I finally got the tick and popped it between my fingernails. End of story. Or so I thought.

I was laughing at the way this big guy started to panic about a little tick on his arm. Then he said, "Hey! There's one on your shirt!" Sure enough, there was a tick on the collar of my T-shirt [and] after a few minutes I felt a "tickle-itch" under my arm. My shirt is off in a nano-second, [and I'm] searching for a bug in my armpit. About that time, my partner thinks he feels something and slams on the brakes. The truck doesn't even get off the road completely before we're both jumping out of the truck, looking at the seats and then our clothes.

The next thing you know, we're feeling tickle-itches everywhere! My partner says to me, "You better look in your drawers." That did it. I panicked. I undid my belt and dropped my jeans to inspect my drawers, and the little bastards were all along my waistband. I yelled some obscenity and in nothing flat I took off all my clothes right there on Highway 395. When I looked up, I saw my partner was also nude as a jaybird, wildly trying to brush off his entire body with his T-shirt, as was I.

Neither of us heard the California Highway Patrol car that pulled up behind us. I can only imagine what it must have been like for this cop seeing two grown men on the side of Highway 395, buck naked, in the middle of some crazed dance, swatting each other and themselves with T-shirts, yelling and screaming like insane escapees from the local crazy-house.

The cop got out of his car and yelled, "What the hell do you two think you're doing?" We both were caught so completely off guard, but we both said at the exact same time, "Ticks!" The cop started laughing, then harder, then even harder. A few cars had passed us by this time and he said, "You better get behind one of those bushes before I have to write you up for indecent exposure." He got in his car laughing, and just drove off.

I looked at my partner, all swat-marked and welted from his rat-tail beating he gave himself, and I told him, "I'm not putting these damn clothes back on!" So we drove all the way back to Orange County in our underwear. And every little thing that touched us caused a mad search for the dome light switch, pulling off the skivvies, looking for yet another tick.

For the next week, anytime we felt even the wind blow, we were crazed with the reaction to tear our clothes off and search ourselves. It was not very funny to us at the time, but it is now. And I can just imagine the story that cop is still telling to this day.

Taking a photo of a jumping tarpon can be an exciting moment. It can also be a painful one when the tarpon is jumping toward you.

In May 1971, Lamar Underwood, editor-in-chief of *Sports Afield* magazine, was fishing on the Parismina River in Costa Rica. In another boat fifty yards away, Tom Paugh, the magazine's saltwater editor, hooked an eighty-pound tarpon.

Underwood grabbed his camera and stood up in his boat, hoping to get a shot of the fish jumping. Suddenly, he heard Paugh yell, "Watch out! He's coming!"

Recalled Underwood, "I remember seeing the line slicing through the water near my boat. Then there was a flash of silver and the next thing I knew I was underwater."

When Underwood surfaced, he saw the guide in his boat wrestling onboard with the thrashing tarpon. The guide won the fight. It was the only tarpon that Paugh or Underwood landed in a week of fishing.

Underwood had a memento of the tarpon encounter— a broken bone in his right foot that forced him to use crutches for a month after his return home.

Joe Schieferstein and his brother John, both of Long Island, were out with three friends in Joe's twenty-one-foot center-console boat, taking part in a shark tournament east of the town of Moriches on September 15, 1985.

Soon Joe hooked a 450-pound mako that had a lot of acrobatic fight in it. As his fellow anglers attached a stand-up harness to him, Joe kept a steady grip on his fifty-pound Penn International. The fish jumped about 300 feet away and a few seconds later it jumped again—this time 150 feet away.

It suddenly became clear to the men onboard that the shark wasn't trying to get away; it was trying to get in the boat. Two of the passengers who had never been shark fishing before but had seen the movie *Jaws* ran for cover toward the bow.

Seconds later, the mako made its third jump—right into the boat and on top of its captor, Joe Schieferstein. "He knocked my brother out," John told the *New York Times*. "He also broke the outboard cover and the rod holders and the leaning post. He really messed up the boat. And he had Joe pinned."

Fortunately, the shark hit the post at such an angle that it was able to flip itself out of the boat. But the mako took Joe's

$700 rod and reel with it. Joe suffered abrasions to his chest—and his pride—but was able to pilot the boat back to Moriches with no rod, no reel, and no fish, but one great fish tale.

The potbelly of an overweight fisherman probably saved his life during a shark attack off the coast of Pahang, Malaysia.

At least, that's the conclusion of Dr. K. Bala, who treated fisherman Razali Ngah. The physician told the Malaysian newspaper the *Star* that the shark's bite would have ripped apart Ngah's intestines and other vital organs if not for the layer of fat around the fisherman's ample midriff.

Ngah and three other fishermen were in the water checking their nets for fish on May 12, 1993, when they saw three sharks approaching. The fishermen presumed that the sharks would attack the fish in the nets, not them. They were wrong.

One of the sharks, measuring about twelve feet, charged Ngah and sank its sharp teeth into his abdomen. "It hung on," he told the *Star*. "I had to use all my strength to push it away."

The shark ripped out a huge section of flesh and then fought its fellow sharks for the human spoils. Meanwhile, Ngah was left with a gaping wound that exposed his intestines. He managed to stagger away and was hauled into his boat by the other fishermen, who rushed him to the hospital. Doctors used skin grafts from his thighs to help heal the wound.

Ngah told the *Star* that even though the attack was horrible, he wouldn't give up net fishing because he had been doing it since he was eight years old.

A Russian fisherman has a tale to tell of the big one that wouldn't get away. But he sure wished it had.

According to a CNN report on January 11, 1996, the unnamed fisherman had caught a tweny-eight-inch pike in the icy waters of the Ivanko Reservoir in Russia. The angler decided to show off his catch to his buddies so he raised the fish above his head and kissed it on the mouth. That wasn't too smart because the fish was still alive.

The pike clamped down hard on the man's nose and wouldn't let go. Even after the guy's friends beheaded the fish, its jaws stayed firmly clenched on his schnozz. The fisherman was taken to a hospital where doctors finally freed him.

A Romanian angler who had just caught the biggest fish of his life lost his catch when an otter bit him on his rear, according to the international news source Ananova.

The otter attacked Razvan Abulboacei from behind as he was fishing in a local river in County Iasi on March 30, 2001. The angler had to go to the hospital for treatment for the bum bite.

Both the fish and the otter escaped.

A fisherman was pulled off his boat by a porpoise and whisked through the water until he let go.

Joseph Deriggs, of Provincetown, Massachusetts, had gone out on the morning of October 11, 1931, in a trap boat with four other men to hand-line for haddock. The boat was anchored near a swift tidal current when Deriggs

felt a powerful pull on his line. At about the same time, the
boat pitched just enough for Deriggs to lose his balance, and
he went overboard. He was so surprised that he forgot to let
go of the line.

His fellow fishermen were just as surprised when they
saw him speeding away toward the open sea. The captain of
the boat, Ulysses Simmons, gunned the engine and was
hardly able to keep up with Deriggs, who still clutched the
line as though his life depended on it. When someone held
out a gaff handle, he let go of the line and was soon pulled
aboard.

The fishermen were wondering what sea creature had
become entangled in the line and taken Deriggs for a tow.
Suddenly, about twenty yards from the boat, a porpoise
poked its head out of the water. According to a contempo-
rary account of the episode, "Deriggs declared that he could

tell from the disgusted expression on its face that the porpoise had been pulling him through the water."

They called it a "Cape Cod sleigh ride," but it had nothing to do with snow or a horse and everything to do with a teenager and a whale.

On June 28, 1948, Frank Cabral and his seventeen-year-old son Frank Junior, both of Provincetown, Massachusetts, started out in their thirty-foot powerboat for their lobster pots. Towed behind them were two dories, one of which had an outboard motor. About three miles out to sea, they anchored the boat and each got into a dory.

They were about one hundred yards apart when Frank Senior spotted a seventy-foot whale that he recognized as the same one that had visited the area the previous two summers and had been nicknamed Willie by him. Suddenly, Willie headed for Frank Junior's dory. Frank Senior yelled a warning to his son but there was little Frank Junior could do.

The whale hit the dory, sending the teenager high into the air. Seconds later, Frank Senior couldn't believe his eyes. There was his son cutting through the water on the back of the whale!

"My boy Frank, so help me, was riding on Willie's back," Frank Senior said later in an account that was published in the *New York Times* the following day. "I was yelling and then I saw Frank stand up and dive into the water. Then Willie sounded. I rowed faster than I ever rowed in my life and I got Frank into my dory. All he had was a cut finger."

Frank Junior's dory was taking water through a hole in its port bow. Father and son removed the outboard motor from the stricken craft, put it on the other dory, and then returned to their big boat. They towed both dories back to port. Stuck to the splinters by the hole of Frank Junior's dory was a piece of whale hide several inches square.

When asked to comment on the extraordinary incident, Frank Junior said, "I tell you when the whale hit my dory it felt like a steam engine. I thought I was a goner. I felt him moving under me. I was on him until I was maybe twenty yards from my dory. Then I stood up and dove."

After hearing the story directly from the father and son, Jack Johnson, editor of the local newspaper, *The Cape Codder*, told the *Times*, "I looked [Frank Senior] in the eye, and all I can say is that Frank Cabral looked me straight back in the eye like an honest man."

While fishing off a dock, Gina Parkinson was filled with anticipation not only of catching a nice bass but also of delivering a healthy child because she was in her final month of pregnancy.

Here's what Parkinson wrote on fishingnetwork.net (reprinted here with permission) about this momentous day:

> I was standing on the dock and, boy, did I get a hit. So I started yelling and screaming, "Oh my God! Oh my God!" because it was a real biggie. But nobody was around except the neighbor two doors down. He heard me screaming and thought I was in labor and called the police. (He was an old man who didn't know what to do.)
>
> The police showed up and, to their surprise, there I was—very pregnant with a very big fish. My husband and parents then showed up at the same time, thinking

Fishing Trip-Ups

I had the baby. My husband was not disappointed when he saw my fish.

Her prize catch made Parkinson so excited that she soon went into labor and delivered a healthy baby the next day.

By the way, the fish weighed more than my baby. I had a seven-pound, nine-ounce baby, but my bass was eight pounds, eleven ounces.

Catch of the Dazed

Bizarre Things Reeled In

ANTHONY JOSHUA WAS FISHING on the banks of the River Wye at Bartonsham in Hertfordshire, England, on November 22, 2001, just as he had done so many times before. Only this time would be different. This time he would be a hero.

"I noticed what looked like a pile of clothes floating by," Joshua later told reporters. "Thinking nothing of it,

I cast off to see if I could catch it. I was lucky on the third time.

"Suddenly these arms rose out of the water. It was incredible. I couldn't believe it when I realized it was a man. I knew I had to get him out. He was blue and shaking violently. I didn't think he had long to live."

Moments earlier a sixty-year-old man had been walking along the riverbank when he slipped and fell into the frigid water. He was unable to swim back to shore because his water-logged clothes had weighed him down and he couldn't fight the current. He was close to death when Joshua hooked the drowning man and brought him to shore, where the angler revived him and then summoned help. A paramedic who had been called to the scene told the press that the man, whose identity wasn't known, would not have survived another minute in the water.

"I'm just glad I was in the right place at the right time," said Joshua. "The bloke is alive and I'm delighted I could help."

While fishing on vacation in northern Norway, Jens Ovesen, of Denmark, slipped on the side of a steep bank, plunged into the water, and was being swept downstream on the morning of July 19, 2001.

Expert fisherman Kjell Wilhelmsen, of Norway, was nearby and saw his fellow angler's predicament. "I saw him slip, try to get up and then slip again," Wilhelmsen told the Swedish newspaper *Expressen*. "I knew the river's currents are strong and that he would soon be pulled in much deeper. It looked as though he had been paralyzed, and I knew I had to act fast."

Wilhelmsen ran along the shoreline and then cast his line at the flailing fisherman, who was about ten yards away. The Norwegian snagged him with the first cast when his hook caught on Ovesen's pants and then reeled him to shore. Fortunately, Ovesen didn't need hospital treatment. Later that day, he treated his rescuer to a bottle of cognac and a new fishing reel as a thank-you.

Wilhelmsen joked that catching the 246-pound Ovesen was a new personal record. "My previous best catch was 12.5 kilograms [27.5 pounds]. I caught it near the spot where I got the Dane."

Fisherman Armand Grenot made the greatest catch of his life on April 18, 1961—he hooked a little boy and saved him from drowning with a single perfect cast.

Grenot was fishing from a bridge above the Cher River in Tours, France, when he heard shouts of alarm coming from a group of children who were playing below him on the riverbank. Three-year-old Claude Latapy had slipped, rolled down the bank, and plunged into the water. The current quickly swept the child out of everyone's reach.

"I couldn't do anything but watch in horror at first," Grenot later told the press. "I was too far away to jump in and swim to him. And I just couldn't think how to help."

Then a man dived into the water, but the current pushed him to the other side of the river before he was able to reach the boy. Another young man went in but he got a cramp in his leg and almost drowned himself. In the meantime, Claude was drifting further away.

"I saw then that there was just one chance to reach him before he went under," said Grenot. "I knew I had to fish him out."

Grenot, who had become an expert at casting from his years of fishing on the Cher, aimed carefully. He whipped back his fishing rod and sent the hook and lead sinker shooting across the water. The hook landed on the little boy and miraculously snagged his jacket.

"I began to reel him in very carefully," said Grenot. "The boy was unconscious by this time, so he couldn't struggle, which was a good thing. The current was strong, but the nylon line had enough strength to hold against it.

"As I reeled him in, I walked off the bridge to the bank of the river and we were able to reach the little boy and pull him in."

Claude, who was still unconscious but breathing, was quickly revived.

Said Grenot, "I won't ever have a more important catch in my entire life."

Amazingly, just ten days earlier, a similar scene played out in England.

While fishing on the banks of a river near Hamilton, England, sixteen-year-old angler John Cutshaw snagged what he thought was an old jacket floating on the surface. As he reeled it in, his jaw dropped in shock. It was no jacket, but the limp body of a baby boy.

Cutshaw frantically brought the unconscious boy onto the bank. The baby, twenty-month-old Samuel Roddel, had wandered away from his family's riverfront home and had fallen into the water. By the time his parents had realized he was missing, Cutshaw had reeled him in. Samuel's parents raced down to the bank and tried desperately for ten minutes to resuscitate him. To their everlasting relief, Samuel started breathing again. He was taken to the hospital where he was treated and released.

For Cutshaw, no fish will ever match his lifesaving catch.

A skillful cast by angler S. J. Oakes, of St. Petersburg, Florida, saved the life of Mrs. S. C. George of Detroit on February 21, 1929.

The woman had waded into the Gulf along a St. Petersburg beach when the current pulled her into eight feet of water. Unable to swim, she screamed and began to go under. Her husband swam after her, but the current shoved him away from her.

Hearing her cries for help, Oakes, who was fishing nearby, cast his line at her. The large hook caught her in the hand, and the fisherman reeled her onto the shore. Mrs. George, whose husband made it safely back to the beach unaided, was taken to the hospital where the hook was removed.

Paul Johanns found the key to fishing—but it wasn't where he thought it would be.

One day in 1968, Johanns, of Osage, Iowa, was fishing on the banks of the Cedar River and hooked a big catfish, but it got away. When he was finished for the day, he realized that his car keys were missing. He figured that they must have fallen out of his shirt pocket when he was leaning over trying to land the fish.

A week later, he returned to the same fishing spot, and this time he successfully landed a good-sized catfish. He brought it home and started cleaning it. When he cut open its stomach, he discovered inside an amazing surprise—his missing car keys!

Sheriff's deputies Russell Mize and John Townsend called off their fishing trip after Mize lost his wallet while they were getting their boat launched at a marina near Sarasota, Florida, on August 18, 1967. Mize was upset because he lost his money, fishing license, driver's license, and credit cards not to mention his badge.

Back home a few hours later, Mize was still stewing over his misfortune when he received a phone call from a stranger named Jurgen K. Feuerherd who had an interesting piece of information that would change the deputy's mood considerably.

Feuerherd and his sister were fishing near a jetty that led to the Gulf of Mexico when they spotted a wallet floating on the water. They managed to snare it and saw that it belonged to Mize. They returned it soggy but intact.

An angler in a boat on Montana's Holter Lake had the fight of his life, not realizing that on the other end of the line was a scuba diver who literally had the fight of *his* life.

On September 1, 1985, Rod Johnson, of Great Falls, Montana, and his brother Chuck Spencer, of Helena, were scuba diving, looking for lures that had been lost when fishing lines broke. Their families were in boats at the surface, warning fishermen away.

On one dive fifty-five feet deep in the lake, Johnson later told the Associated Press, he felt something bite him on the leg near his ankle. He reached back to find out what had bit him and caught his hand on a hook that was attached to a taut fishing line. Before he could deal with the fact that his hand was now hooked to his ankle, the line somehow yanked off his face mask and then pulled his regulator, which supplied air, from his mouth. Johnson managed to put the mask back on and retrieve the mouthpiece. But now he had another problem. Because he was hooked, he was being towed upward feet first.

When Johnson reached the surface, the fisherman was still reeling him in. "Hey, you got hooks in me!" Johnson yelled. The shocked angler stopped reeling.

Johnson started sinking and was unable to swim because his hand was still hooked to his ankle. The fisherman hauled him to the surface, freed the hook from Johnson, and then took off without identifying himself or offering any apologies or further assistance.

Meanwhile, Johnson suffered a severe case of the bends because he had been dragged to the surface too quickly. As a result, he had to spend several hours in the nearest recompression chamber 500 miles away at a Seattle hospital.

Fishing was pretty poor in Tennessee's Chickamauga Lake for Earl Wall of Chattanooga on September 22, 1962.

He was about to give up when he noticed some bubbles surfacing near a little cove and figured they came from a carp. He motored his boat to the spot and dragged a light lure through the bubbles a couple of times. That's when he snared the most surprising catch of his life.

"All of a sudden right out from under my boat, up popped this scuba diver," Wall recalled. "He took a long look at me through his mask, scowled, and then submerged as fast as he came up." Wall decided it wasn't a good day for fishing and went home.

In 1996, the skipper of a charter fishing boat put out his trolling lures in an area popular among scuba divers in the waters off Cabo San Lucas, Mexico. His client immediately got a hookup and began battling what he thought was going to be a great catch.

A half hour later, the angler reeled to the surface an angry scuba diver who had been hooked in the back of his wetsuit in a spot he couldn't reach. The skipper carefully released him and headed for deeper water.

"It was the biggest diver ever caught in Cabo San Lucas," claimed Guillermo Gamio, who managed a small fleet of fishing boats there. "It was a world record, like a 250-pound diver."

Angler Ernest Hinman couldn't believe his eyes as he guided his motorboat two miles off Coney Island. What he first thought was a huge fish or a capsized boat turned out to be a black-and-white Holstein bull paddling strongly in the Atlantic Ocean, but showing signs of exhaustion.

So Hinman caught it. Actually, he fashioned fishing line around the bull's horns and began towing it toward land, all the while wondering who would ever believe that he went fishing and came back with a live bull.

The strange saga began on July 5, 1930, when a champion bull from Pennsylvania was being transported in a crate on the municipal ferryboat *Nassau* from Staten Island to the steamship piers in Brooklyn. The 1,200-pound bull was supposed to be shipped to Puerto Rico for breeding purposes.

But shortly after the *Nassau* left the docks at St. George on Staten Island, the animal broke free from its crate. While chasing a couple of crew members, the snorting and bellowing animal slipped and plunged off the ferryboat and into the water.

Captain Michael Nolan summoned help. Four police launches, two Coast Guard vessels, and a tugboat searched the Narrows and Lower Bay for the seagoing bull. But there was no trace of the animal, and authorities officially listed it as drowned.

What they didn't know until later in the day was that the bull had swum seven miles in the bay and been caught by a fisherman who was towing it to Seagate on the western edge of Coney Island.

Unfortunately for Hinman the instant the bull reached shallow water and felt the bottom, the animal went on the warpath again and charged the angler's boat. Hinman quickly turned his boat around and dragged the beast out into deeper water and then to Brooklyn, where he tied the animal to a bulkhead in shallow water, and called police. It took a dozen men with ropes to drag the bull out of the water and into a truck that took it to an animal shelter. The bull was tired but otherwise unhurt.

As for Hinman, he had a fishing story to tell that was a lot of bull.

Catch of the Dazed

It was the doggonest thing that fishermen Walter Jarka and George Walko had ever seen.

Early in the morning on July 6, 1969, the two saltwater anglers from Carteret, New Jersey, embarked in their twenty-one-foot boat to troll for flounder, blues, and stripers. But they didn't have much luck so they headed farther out to sea, about six miles from New Jersey's Sandy Hook peninsula. They weren't getting any bites there either, but about noon they began getting barks.

Jarka and Walko couldn't believe their ears, but it definitely sounded like a dog barking off their starboard bow. They scanned the horizon and sure enough they spotted a canine dog-paddling in the chilly Atlantic. They edged their boat toward the yelping animal and then stretched a grappling pole to it and brought the dog close enough so they could grab it and pull it into their boat. The dog was a charcoal-colored miniature French poodle that looked in remarkably good shape for swimming in the ocean miles from land.

"What gets me," Jarka told the *New York Daily News*, "is there were no other boats in the area. The dog must have swum out." Whether or not the unidentified canine chose to go for a long swim, had been swept out to sea, or had fallen off his master's boat, the two anglers had a shaggy-dog tale to tell.

A commercial fisherman in his boat off the coast of Maine made a ghoulish catch while hauling in his net—a coffin with a body in it.

On June 27, 2002, the man was fishing off Mount Desert Island when he called the Coast Guard to report that he had caught "a metal box with handles on the side." Authorities traced the coffin to a funeral home in Maine that had arranged a burial at sea two years earlier. The coffin was eventually returned to its final watery resting place.

The fisherman gave new meaning to the term "dead in the water."

Anglers Michael Nagy and Jeremy Lloyd had no idea just how dangerous a catch they had during their fishing outing on the banks of the Schuylkill River on August 18, 2002.

They had found a rusted, two-foot-long rocket in a shallow area of the river in Berks County about forty miles northwest of Philadelphia. Considering it was the most impressive catch either of them had ever fished out of the river, the two anglers posed for photographs with the rocket before taking it to a nearby police station.

That's when they learned it was a live military rocket.

"It was confirmed as an active military device, an RPG [rocket-propelled grenade]," said West Pottsgrove police officer Steven Ziegler. "It had the firing pin still in. That's how we knew it was live." The military-issue surface-to-air rocket was designed to be launched out of a weapon such as a grenade launcher. The Montgomery County Sheriff's Bomb Disposal Unit, which detonated the device at a remote location, said it was unclear how the rocket ended up in the river.

As for the two anglers, they were grateful their day fishing didn't turn into a blast.

William Simmons was a thirty-one-year-old unemployed longshoreman whose wife was expecting their first baby. So what did Simmons do? He went fishing with his buddies—and it was a good thing he did too.

On August 6, 1958, Simmons, of Baltimore, was fishing in Chesapeake Bay near Annapolis when he caught a rockfish. But this was no ordinary rockfish. This one was tagged and had a name, Diamond Jim III. It had been put into the bay by a local brewery, which offered a diamond worth $25,000 to anyone who caught the tagged fish.

While fishing off Fishers Island on May 15, 1924, Captain Frank Thompson, of New London, Connecticut, landed a complete automobile chassis. It was thought that the chassis accidentally had fallen off a steamer that was transporting car parts.

An angler in Hong Kong reeled in a catch that caught the eye of the police.

The twenty-year-old man had dropped his line off a pier in Kowloon on March 8, 2003, when it became hooked on what he thought was a large fish. He reeled it in and discovered he had snared a thirty-three-pound bag of marijuana.

He called police, who believed the pot had been hurled into the sea by smugglers whose boat was being intercepted by marine authorities. The street value of the grass was estimated at $173,000.

An eleven-year-old fisherman looking for crayfish reeled in the most impressive catch of his young life—a bank bag filled with $2,000 in soaked checks.

Devonte Martinez, of Superior, Colorado, was fishing along the banks of Coal Creek on June 9, 2003, when he hooked three bank bags. Two of them were empty but the other contained the checks, which were written out to the Imagine Foundation charity.

"I thought someone accidentally lost the bags out the window of a car," Devonte told the Associated Press. "I know what it feels like; I once lost two dollars when I was riding to the video game store."

His catch was taken to Boulder County authorities, who said the bags had been stolen the night before from a Boulder restaurant, where the Imagine Foundation had held a fund-raiser. The thief apparently took the cash out of the bags—about $2,600—and threw away the rest.

Members of the foundation, which provides services and housing for people with developmental disabilities, thanked Devonte and gave him a fleece vest and food and entertainment coupons. The restaurant gave him a gift certificate.

A short while later, Devonte went back fishing along Coal Creek, still looking for crayfish to catch.

Fishing in the Rockaway River near Pine Brook, New Jersey, on August 12, 1911, James Gaffigan hooked a canoe. He and his fishing buddy pulled the boat up from the bottom of the river and discovered a locked wooden box under the seat. It was heavy and when they shook it, they could hear rattling.

Thinking it might be some kind of treasure, they planned to take the box home and open it up. On the way home, they stopped at Lewandoski's Hotel for dinner in Pine Brook. Not wanting to leave the box in the car, they brought it in with them and set it on the table.

One of the restaurant employees noticed that the box resembled one filled with silverware that had been stolen seven years earlier and called police. When the cops arrived, the anglers told their story of how they found the box and agreed to have it opened. Police busted the lock and everyone in the restaurant let out a shout. Inside was all the stolen silverware.

On August 10, 1944, Captain Paul Campbell, of Martha's Vineyard, was trolling off Block Island in his thirty-eight-foot fishing boat, *Little David*, when he felt the deck shudder beneath him and his boat began moving backward.

Campbell was convinced that he had hooked a whale. Still moving backward while its screw churned futilely, *Little David* began to sink at the stern. The gunwale dipped toward the water, forcing Campbell to cut loose his fishing line to save his vessel from foundering.

As the craft lurched free, Campbell heard a loud whoosh and saw that it wasn't a whale that had tangled with his line. It was a United States navy submarine, which was surfacing by the *Little David*'s stern. Like a bluefin that had tossed the hook, the sub went merrily on its way.

Catch of the Dazed

Branko Prascevic was at his favorite fishing hole in the Lim River near Plav, Yugoslavia, on September 14, 1966, but he wasn't catching any trout.

He was about to call it a day when he made one final cast. To his surprise, he had a strike even before the hook had hit the water. It was a fight to haul in his catch—because he had snared an eagle that was in its nest in a tree overhead.

"It took a while to release him," he said. "That's not the kind of catch I want. I prefer fish."

While fishing in a large stream near Trento, Italy, Niccolo Simion reeled in a mountain goat. No kidding.

On August 31, 1963, Simion, thirty-eight, had just lowered his line when a goat came hurtling down from an overhanging ledge, barely missing him, and landed in the water.

The angler used his line to bring the goat to the banks of the stream, but it was already dead from the fall. Nevertheless, Simion didn't lie when he told his friends he had caught an eighty-pounder.

The codfish has a monstrous mouth in proportion to its body, and is one of the ocean's most voracious eaters. It will swallow most anything that can fit in its mouth.

The cod off the coast of Maine aren't particular about what they eat.

In 1929, three fishermen from Islesboro, Maine, caught a seventy-pound codfish in outer Penobscot Bay, and when they cut open its stomach they pulled out a sealed bottle of liquor. Apparently, the bottle was from cargo jettisoned by rumrunners who were being chased by the feds.

The same year, M. J. Flaherty, of Portland, Maine, discovered an empty Budweiser bottle inside a cod's stomach. A few days later, he was dressing a big cod when he found a large jackknife, with its blade open, in the fish's tummy.

When Fred Orne cut open a thirty-six-pounder that he had caught in Casco Bay, Maine, he pulled out a blackened briar pipe.

Sometimes the cod taketh away and then giveth. In 1879, two crew members aboard the schooner *Willie G*, which sailed out of Boothbay Harbor, accidentally broke off the handle of their water jug so they tossed the handle overboard. They gave the broken jug to the ship's cook to use as a container. A month later, while fishing in the same waters from the same schooner, one of the crewmen caught a cod. When he opened its stomach, he pulled out a broken handle. To his amazement, it fit the broken jug exactly. The crew donated the jug to a museum in Boothbay Harbor.

Codfish seem to have a taste for jewelry. Homer Le Blanc of North Sydney, Nova Scotia, pulled from the stomach of a big steak cod a bracelet set with twelve small diamonds. While dressing cod, Elmer Grant of Small Point, Maine, took a woman's small wristwatch and a plain gold ring from two separate fish on the same day.

Apparently, Maine cod aren't the only sea creatures with an attraction to jewelry. Cliff Island lobsterman Joe Estes reported bringing up a three-pound lobster from one of his traps. Clasped on its tail just above its flippers was an expensive gold bracelet.

Catch of the Dazed

Joseph Cross, Jr., lost his $400 college class ring in July 1980, while sailing during a storm on the Chesapeake Bay. The gold ring fell off his finger into the water and he gave up hope of ever seeing it again.

But eighteen months later, the ring was back with its owner—thanks to a good Samaritan and a fish that didn't get away.

Apparently, a bluefish—an aggressive feeder that will gulp down anything that sparkles—had swallowed the lost ring and then sometime later was caught and sold to a fish market. During processing at a plant 140 miles from the bay, the ring tumbled out of the fish's stomach and went unnoticed when the garbage was collected. Somehow the ring fell out when the garbage was picked up.

In December 1981, Coleman Maddox, a consulting engineer, spotted the ring on the ground and noted that it was a class ring of a graduate from the University of

Virginia, his alma mater. Jotting down the engraved initials, date, fraternity, and other markings on the ring, Maddox searched yearbooks and university directories in search of its owner.

Several days later, he found Cross's name and called him.

"At first I thought he was pulling my leg," Cross told United Press International.

Satisfied he had found the owner, Maddox sent Cross the ring. It was still in good condition.

When a Boston fisherman found a ring in the stomach of a codfish that he had caught in October 1934, he took it to authorities who told the press, which spread the word about the discovery.

A week later, the Reverend E. T. Drake of the First Presbyterian Church of Orange, Texas, claimed it was the ring he had lost while swimming off Corpus Christi, Texas, twenty-eight years earlier.

The minister said he had read of the finding of the ring in the newspapers and contacted police in Boston. The ring bore the inscription "Pat D," the abbreviation of his mother's name, Patricia Drake.

Cod have been known to live more than thirty years, but it sure is a long swim from the Gulf of Mexico to the fishing grounds off the coast of Massachusetts.

Hooks, Lines, and Stinkers

Odd Fish Scraps

CLARK MILLS WAS A MASTER BUILDER of wood-construction boats in Clearwater, Florida. Known as "Captain of the Seawall," Clark retired in the 1980s and put together a booklet of stories he compiled about the good old days and the salty dogs he met.

One of his favorite true yarns was about the time a captain of a charter boat took a husband and wife out on a fishing trip. The captain quickly realized that the woman was the most overbearing, most obnoxious person he had ever had the displeasure of meeting. When the husband suggested that, for an extra five dollars, the captain fix it so the woman would get seasick, the captain readily agreed.

It just so happened the waves were fairly active out on the Gulf of Mexico so the captain eased the boat across the swells, causing the boat to pitch and roll. It didn't take long for the woman to lean over the railing and heave her guts out—including her false teeth.

Two weeks later, after another fishing trip with a different party, the captain was cleaning a grouper caught by one of the anglers when, to his amazement, he found an upper plate in perfect condition. Convinced that it was the bossy woman's, he wrapped up the teeth and sent them to her with an explanation of the astonishing million-to-one chance of how he found them.

Back came a thank-you note saying the false teeth weren't hers, but she appreciated them anyway because they fit much better than the ones she lost.

Anglers were baffled in September 1917, when fish in the Delaware River near Easton, Pennsylvania, appeared to be dancing. As one angler noted, "It looked as though these fish were moving to ragtime."

Charles Snyder, of the Zoological Park in the Bronx, went to investigate. What he discovered left fishermen laughing among themselves.

At one certain spot just below Sand Island, he found more than a dozen fish zigzagging about, circling in and out, but never getting beyond ten feet of any given point. Back and forth they went, keeping time near the surface of the water, and sometimes bumping into each other.

"There were large and small fish in the group," Snyder later told the *New York Times*. "Little fish knocked against the big fellows and the big ones pushed aside the smaller ones, all in evident great good humor. There was one big fellow who appeared to lead the crazy parade. He would pause every once in a while with his head pointed toward a certain spot on shore. The others would go circling about in their merry way until one would knock against the big fellow and then he too would go off careering along in the lead of the bunch.

"Several fishermen stood with me on the bank and watched the antics of the fish. One man told me they were not only crazy, but were tame. To prove it, he waded out from shore a little distance and when the fish dance headed his way, he stooped and picked up one of the dancers. 'He's a tame one,' said the fisherman, handing the passive fish to me. When I got a whiff of that fish's breath, I knew just what the trouble was.

"The fish were drunk!"

Snyder then tried to figure out how respectable fish in the Delaware River had become so stewed.

He solved the mystery after learning a federal inspector had paid an unexpected visit to a nearby brewery a few days earlier. Finding the beer was below standards, the inspector ordered eighty barrels of the suds dumped into the river. But instead of pouring the contents into the Delaware where the beer would quickly be diluted by the currents, the brewers emptied the barrels within ten feet of the riverbank. Most of the beer seeped into a depression between the rocks and then gradually trickled into the river, forming several pools close by Sand Island.

"When the fish wanted to go on a spree, they entered one of these beer-polluted pools or swam to the point where the beer was entering the river and drank directly from the flow," explained Snyder, who wrote an official report of his findings, which was called "The Great Fish Jag of the Delaware River."

Fish were getting sloshed to the gills in Tennessee's Mulberry Creek on July 16, 1987. Suckers, minnows, and other fish were diving while intoxicated after a broken pipe at the famous Jack Daniel's Distillery leaked 13,800 gallons of whiskey into the creek near Lynchburg.

"As much as a mile downstream you could pick out the smell as being Jack Daniel's liquor," said biologist Dick

Williams of the Tennessee Wildlife Resources Agency. "And those fish downstream were swimming kind of sluggish."

It's not known how many fish ended up fried.

Drunken fish were dying, presumably happily, by the thousands near Lawrenceburg, Kentucky, after a seven-story warehouse burned to the ground on May 9, 2000, spilling thousands of gallons of Wild Turkey bourbon into the Kentucky River.

The warehouse, owned by Boulevard Distillers and Importers, Inc., held more than seventeen thousand barrels of bourbon, some aged for fifteen years. Each barrel contained about fifty-three gallons. State biologists said that when the Wild Turkey leaked into the river, microscopic bacteria and algae feeding on the sugar in the alcohol sucked all the oxygen out of the river in a plume that slowly wound its way downstream. As a result, hundreds of thousands of fish weighing almost eighty thousand pounds were killed—an ecological disaster that affected thirty species, including nine sport fish species and sixteen species of commercial value.

The Kentucky Department of Fish and Wildlife Resources (KDFWR) originally billed Boulevard Distillers $499,739 for the value of the dead fish, but the company balked. However, on January 5, 2001, both sides reached a settlement. The Wild Turkey Distillery, a subsidiary of Boulevard Distillers, paid the KDFWR $256,000 for loss of fish and wildlife. The department began restocking fish along the section of the Kentucky River from Frankfort to Carrollton.

Hopefully, no more fish will be pickled in bourbon.

Other than torturing and killing countrymen who opposed him, one of Iraqi dictator Saddam Hussein's favorite pastimes was fishing, but not with rod and reel. He used hand grenades.

French filmmaker Joel Soler learned of Saddam's fishing technique while spending two months in Iraq in 2000 making a documentary about the vicious, egocentric tyrant. The film, called *Uncle Saddam*, focused on the Butcher of Baghdad's personal eccentricities, including the way he fished.

Soler managed to smuggle out of Iraq footage of Saddam tossing a grenade into a pond. "He loved to fish," Soler told the BBC. "But he loved to fish with grenades. So when he went fishing, he took a scuba diver and a grenade, and he threw the grenade into the water and suddenly you had hundreds of dead fish." The diver would then go in and retrieve all the fish.

An angler who forgot to buy a ticket for a fishing derby caught the biggest fish, but lost out on the $30,000 jackpot.

Every year since 1986, Alaska's Kenai Peninsula has played host to the Homer Jackpot Halibut Derby in which hundreds of anglers who buy derby tickets qualify for cash prizes for catching the largest halibut and tagged halibut during the halibut season.

In 2000, Tim Collins, of Anchorage, Alaska, was on his way to buy a $7.00 ticket when he stopped off at a fast-food restaurant for a sandwich. By the time he finished, he forgot about the ticket. He later caught a four-hundred-pound halibut that would have netted him the grand prize of $31,820. In fact, it would have been the largest catch ever in the derby's history.

"What can I say?" Collins shrugged. "I really wish I had picked up a ticket. But I got myself a nice Subway sandwich."

Fellow angler Clayton McDowell would have experienced a similar fate in 2002 if it hadn't been for his wife Cindy. On the day the couple got ready to go fishing, Cindy reminded Clayton about the derby. "I wasn't too happy about getting up at four-thirty in the morning, so when my wife said, 'We need derby tickets,' I thought, 'Yeah, right,'" recalled McDowell, of Eagle River, Alaska. He had never won anything before and had no illusions of winning the derby, but he bought derby tickets for each of them anyway.

Later that day, he reeled in a 347-pound halibut that turned out to be the largest catch of the derby, earning him $48,675.

While fishing in a surfcasting contest in Auckland, New Zealand, on January 2, 1971, angler Robert Hunga caught a snapper. He didn't have a bite the rest of the day. Figuring his snapper was much too small to even be considered for a prize, he took it home before finding out the results of the tournament.

He broiled his snapper and ate it for dinner. It turned out to be the most expensive fish he ever ate.

Not until the next morning did he learn his snapper was the only catch of the contest—and would have earned him a first-place prize of $250.

Whenever Pedro de Andres y Llorens went fishing, he brought along his rod, reel, tackle box, bait—and, of course, his three pigeons.

Throughout the 1960s, the angler, an industrialist from Calencia de Alcantara, Spain, kept his wife informed of his whereabouts and fishing success by using his pet carrier pigeons. One was released when he arrived at his destination, another to report to her on his fishing luck, and a third to inform her when he was returning home.

The townspeople of Patchogue, Long Island, were saddened when authorities declared that two local clam fishermen had drowned during a storm in July 1913.

Jack Ryan and Henry Gill were last seen heading out in their sharpie, a flat-bottomed boat with a sail. Their sharpie was found two days after a storm, floating bottom up near Fire Island. Authorities searched the shoreline and waters off Long Island for days for the bodies without success before ruling the two fishermen had died.

Two weeks after the men were reported missing, the people of Patchogue turned out for an aquatic funeral ceremony. A minister at the water's edge told

how two young lives had been snatched by the remorse-
less sea. The men's friends, who were dressed in black,
rowed a few hundred yards offshore and dropped flowers
into the water.

For days afterward, all anyone could talk about was
the drowning of Ryan and Gill and of all the other fishermen who had met a similar fate.

Eight months later, on March 29, 1914, a man who
looked exactly like Jack Ryan walked into Farrell's
Restaurant, causing patrons to gasp. "What's the matter
with you?" asked the man. "Do you take me for a
ghost?"

The shocked patrons nodded. One brave soul
went up to him and pinched him to determine that

the visitor was not a specter. The man was, in fact, Jack Ryan.

"Good heavens!" shouted one of the townies. "How did you get here? You're supposed to be dead."

After Ryan learned of his "drowning" and Patchogue's tribute to him and his buddy, he explained what had happened. "When we were out on the bay, Gill and I got a notion that we would like to travel a little. Clam fishing was dull, so we thought we would go to New York. We left the sharpie at Bay Shore, and I guess it floated over to Fire Island Beach during the storm. After we got to New York, Gill started for New Jersey and I went down South Carolina way. The other day things got dull there and I thought I would come back and try clam fishing again."

It used to be possible to catch ready-to-eat fish in Yellowstone National Park. Well, almost ready-to-eat.

In the late 1800s and early 1900s, Yellowstone anglers often fished for Yellowstone cutthroat trout near one of the park's hot springs. After pulling a fish from the water, the angler would drop the still-hooked fish into the hot spring. Minutes later he would pull the fish out cooked and ready for eating, according to discovertheoutdoors.com. This practice was outlawed in 1912.

While most anglers buy farm-raised worms at the bait shop, a few self-reliant fishermen in the south still get their bait the old-fashioned way—by fiddling, snoring, grunting, doodling, or calling up the slimy creatures from the ground.

The Mecca for worm fiddling is Caryville, Florida, near the Alabama border, which held its first annual worm-fiddling contest in 1974. Just fifteen miles away in Alabama, the Annual Geneva River Festival has been holding a worm-fiddling contest of its own since the 1980s.

To call up a worm, a person drives a one- or two-foot stake, known as a "stob," into the ground and then rubs a "pusher," such as a brick, an old piece of iron, or an ax head, across the stake. This rhythmic action sends vibrations into the ground that cause the worms to surface. North Carolinians tend to call up worms by sticking a pitchfork into the ground and twanging the handle.

Worm fiddling has become a lost art, according to worm maestro Jack Palmer, who dreamed up the annual Caryville contest. Fiddling worms was a way of life, like hunting and fishing, when he was growing up. "There were no bait shops, so if you wanted to fish, you sure enough had to get your own worms," he once told reporters. "Shoot, when I was a little bitty boy, I could fill me a gallon bucket in no time. I used to get sixteen-inch and eighteen-inch worms."

The best time for worm fiddling is early morning or late afternoon when the ground is cooler and worms are shallow. The best spot is slightly damp earth in a shady swamp.

Demonstrating his technique for Jeff Klinkenberg of the *St. Petersburg Times*, Palmer drove a white pine stob into the ground. Then, like an artist playing Beethoven's Violin Concerto, he rubbed the ax head against the stob, creating squeaks, grunts, and rumbles that shook a fifteen-foot radius. Palmer kept changing the angle of the ax head to get different tones, sometimes stopping to pour sand on the top of the stob to create a grittier pitch.

Wrote Klinkenberg, "Suddenly, on the ground surrounding Jack Palmer, it happened: Earthworms squirmed into the sunlight. If worms had hands and ears, those hands would have been covering ears. Doing everything but begging for mercy, the worms writhed in what can only be described as agony.

"'Them worms don't want to go back in the ground,' said Palmer. 'They sure enough don't. Worm fiddling, it just drives 'em crazy.'"

If you like to hunt for worms for bait, make sure you know the law. Here, for example, is an excerpt from a 1997 issue of the New York State Conservation Officer magazine entitled "Rules and Regulations Regarding the Hunting of Worms":

1996.1 No person shall take worms by means other than legal hunting. The use of motor vehicles, seine nets in mud puddles, bicycles, mopeds, roller blades, electronic calls, electrodes, English starlings, explosives, trained woodcock, firearms or longbows is strictly forbidden.

1996.2 No person shall take or possess a female worm.

1996.3 No person shall possess a worm decoy.

1996.4 No person shall hunt worms over bait.

1996.5 No person shall herd or use a track dog while hunting worms.

(Yes, the article was written tongue-in-cheek.)

The world's greatest collection of antique tackle is now housed in the Oklahoma Aquarium, a thirty-four-acre educational aquatic facility in Tulsa.

The extensive collection was donated by Bassmaster's antique tackle and lure expert Karl White and is showcased inside the four thousand-square-foot Karl and Beverly White National Fishing Tackle Museum, one of many unique exhibits housed at the aquarium.

White's exhibit is valued at $4 million and consists of nearly thirty thousand pieces. Among the prize items are the first outboard gasoline engine and the first Skeeter bass boat to roll off the famed boatmaker's production line. White's tackle collection includes a Pflueger Flying Hellgrammite valued at $7,000. The exhibit also shows off a George Snyder brass bait-casting reel (circa 1820) valued at $50,000 and one of only eight ever made.

The collection is so vast that it took museum curators seven months to photograph and catalog each piece, from popping bugs to one of the first pairs of sunglasses. It took White fifty years to complete the collection, and he could have sold it for millions of dollars. But he told reporters he donated the collection to the Oklahoma Aquarium so it will always be available to the public and stay complete in his home state.

"There's not another one like it and never will be," White said. "I could have sold it to Japan, and it would have gone to Japan. But Oklahoma is where it belongs and where it will stay."

In the highest price ever paid for an antique lure, a private collector shelled out a reported $92,000 in 2003 for a 1910 wooden Heddon Night-Radiant Moonlight bait.

Only about ten are known to exist. This particular one was in very good condition and had retained all its finish, unlike similar baits that tend to lose their luminous paint. Not only that but the expensive lure still had its white box and paperwork. According to experts, antique lures are worth more if they come with the original box and paperwork.

James Heddon & Sons was founded in 1894 in Dowagiac, Michigan, when James Heddon began carving frog lures out of broom handles. He started making wooden lures colored with many layers of thick paint and equipped with glass eyes. Eventually, he ran a factory that turned out fishing lures, rods, reels, fish decoys, and other products. A family company until 1955, it is now owned and operated by Pradco.

Fish reared in hatcheries are learning how to cope in the wild—through training videos.

Hatchery fish are reared in a protected environment with a regular supply of food and no predators. As a result, they face a tough chance of survival when they are released into oceans and rivers to replenish diminished stocks. According to the BBC, most of them die within the first two days and fewer than 5 percent make it to adulthood.

But in 2001 British scientists began devising training videos for hatchery fish that show their species being devoured by a predator. Seeing the videos helps the inexperienced fish learn to survive.

Group training for fish is also proving to be effective. Scientists take an adult fish from the wild and place it in a school of hatchery fish. Then they put a predator behind a transparent but porous screen. From the reactions of the experienced fish and the sight and smell of the predator, the inexperienced fish learn to flee.

Said Cullum Brown, of Cambridge University's department of animal behavior, "Even some very short-lived preliminary exposure to predators makes a significant impact on their chances of survival once released."

The first fishing manual ever published in English was purportedly written by a woman over five hundred years ago.

In 1496, Dame Juliana Berners, prioress of the Benedictine abbey of Sopwell in England, handwrote *Treatise of Fishing with an Angle* (or in Old English, *A Treatyse of Fysshynge wyth an Angle*). The book was published more than 150 years before Izaak Walton, the father of sportfishing, published his famous *The Compleat Angler*.

Although some question her authorship, Berners occupies a similar place in angling literature to that accorded Chaucer in English literature. Dame Juliana's *Treatyse* is one of the oldest works on fishing and many of its words are as true today as they were back in the fifteenth century. For example, she said you should fish ". . . principally for your enjoyment and the health of your body and, more especially, of your soul" and that "the sport of angling is the best way of bringing a man into a merry frame of mind."

In her book, she gave instructions on all facets of fishing, including how to make a telescopic rod, how to braid horsehair into fishing line, and to how to catch fish near waterfalls.

In arguably the greatest fish tale of all time, British seaman James Bartley was swallowed whole by a whale, spent two days in its stomach—and lived to tell about it.

The astounding story of this modern-day Jonah was reported in publications throughout the world, including the *New York Times* and *New York World*.

According to reports, Bartley, thirty-five, was a crewman aboard the whaling ship *Star of the East*, which was hunting whales off the Falkland Islands in February 1891. When a sixty-foot-long sperm whale was spotted, two rowboats, including one carrying Bartley, were dispatched to kill the beast.

Moments after the whale was harpooned, its twelve-foot tail smashed into Bartley's boat, tossing the crewmen into the water. Whalers from the other rowboat rescued all the men but couldn't find Bartley and returned to the mother ship believing he had drowned.

Meanwhile, the whale died and was tied up next to the ship where the crewmen carved it up over the next thirty-six hours. When they hoisted the stomach on board, they could tell something strange was in it, so they cut it open and were shocked to discover the missing sailor, doubled up and unconscious, inside. They laid Bartley on the deck and dumped saltwater on him until he was revived. But although he was alive, he was acting like a "raving lunatic" and had to be placed under guard in the captain's quarters for a couple of weeks before he regained his senses, recovered from his horrifying ordeal, and resumed his duties.

The first published account in the United States didn't appear until five years later, on April 12, 1896, when the *New York World* ran the story under the headline A MODERN JONAH PROVES HIS STORY, with quotes supposedly from Bartley himself.

Seven months later, on November 22, 1896, the *New York Times* published a similar account with the headline SWALLOWED BY A WHALE. It attributed the original story to "the Mercury of South Yarmouth, England, October, 1891," and gave a detailed description of what it was like to be trapped in the stomach of the whale:

"During the brief sojourn in the whale's belly, Bartley's skin, where it was exposed to the action of the gastric juices, underwent a striking change. His face and hands were bleached to a deadly whiteness, and the skin was wrinkled giving the man the appearance of having been parboiled.

"Bartley affirms that he would probably have lived inside his house of flesh until he starved, for he lost his senses through fright and not from lack of air. He says he remembers the sensation of being lifted into the air by the nose of the whale and of dropping into the water. Then there was a frightful rushing sound, which he believed to be the beating of the water by the whale's tail, then he was encompassed by a fearful darkness, and he felt himself slipping along a smooth passage of some sort that seemed to move and carry him forward. This sensation lasted an instant, then he felt that he had more room. He felt about him, and his hands came in contact with a yielding slimy substance that seemed to shrink from the touch. It finally dawned upon him that he had been swallowed by a whale, and he was overcome by horror at the situation.

"He could breathe, but the heat was terrible. It was not of a scorching, stifling nature, but it seemed to draw out his vitality. He became very weak and grew sick at the stomach. He knew that there was no hope of escape from his strange prison. Death stared him in the face, and he tried to look at it bravely but the awful quiet, the fearful darkness, the horrible knowledge of his environments, and the terrible heat finally overcame him, and he must have fainted, for the next he remembered was being in the captain's cabin.

"Bartley is not a man of a timid nature, but he says that it was many weeks before he could pass a night without having his sleep disturbed with harrowing dreams of angry whales and the horrors of his fearful prison. The skin on the face and hands of Bartley has never recovered its natural appearance. It is yellow and wrinkled, and looks like old parchment. The health of the man does not seem to have been affected by his terrible experience. He is in splendid spirits, and apparently fully enjoys all the blessings of life that come his way."

So, did this really happen?

Sir Francis Fox, a leading member of the British evangelical subculture at the turn of the twentieth century, believed the account. He hoped it would uphold the credibility of the biblical story of Jonah, and wrote in 1924 that Bartley's story was carefully investigated by two scientists, including Henri de Parville, the scientific editor of the *Journal des Debats* of Paris, "well-known as a man of sound judgment and a careful writer." Fox received de Parville's English translation of his probe, which was published in the journal. De Parville concluded "the account given by the captain and the crew of the English whaler is worthy of belief" and added, "I won't allow myself to deny the reality of the adventure."

Edward B. Davis, associate professor of science and history at Messiah College in Grantham, Pennsylvania, researched Bartley's claim and wrote about his findings in the December 1991 issue of the *American Scientific Affiliation*. Davis said he found a 1906 article in the *Expository Times* in London that reprinted a letter from Lloyds of London saying the vessel in the Bartley story, the *Star of the East*, had left Auckland, New Zealand, on December 27, 1890, and arrived in New York on April 17, 1891, which could indeed have placed the ship off the Falkland Islands in February.

However, the *Expository Times* reprinted another letter in 1907 that allegedly came from the wife of John Killam, captain of the ship. She stated flatly that there "is not one word of truth in the whale story. I was with my husband all the years he was in the *Star of the East.* There was never a man lost overboard while my husband was in her. The sailor has told a great sea yarn."

From the Maritime Archives, Davis received copies of the ship's documents, including a list of every member of the crew. Said Davis, "There is no James Bartley on the list, nor anyone of similar name, either for the entire voyage or any part thereof.

"I realized then with finality that there simply was no whale at the end of my line, indeed that there never had been a whale, and that all of this was no more than a fish story, albeit a dandy."